I am a Woman

ELLA MAY MILLER

CHOICE BOOKS

Harrisonburg, Virginia 22801

A Choice Book
Published by Moody Press in special
arrangement with Mennonite Broadcasts.

Choice Books edition published January 1975.

Choice Books are distributed exclusively by Mennonite Broadcasts, Inc., Harrisonburg, Virginia 22801.
The word "Choice" and the corresponding symbol are
registered in the United States Patent Office.

ISBN= 0-8024-3925-X

Printed in The United States of America

Contents

INTRODUCTION

Today's woman is fast losing her femininity, her unique-
ness and her God-ordained role as "helper to man" and
"mother of mankind." As a woman, a Christian woman,
I feel a compelling force driving me on to defend "the
quite possible she," as Phyllis McGinley so cleverly states
it.

In this booklet I present a select few radio messages
given on HEART TO HEART, a radio program especially
for homemakers.

These messages are a constant challenge to me to be
a better twentieth century woman.

I hope they do the same for you.

For happier hearts and homes,

ELLA MAY MILLER

1

NOT SECOND-RATE MAN

OVER THE ENTRANCE to Paine Hall, the music building at Harvard, are engraved the words, "To charm, to strengthen and to teach, these are the three great words of might."

These are also the predominate functions of woman.

The noted anthropologist, Ashley Montague, says that women are "gentler, kinder, warmer, more sympathetic, more understanding, more co-operative" than men. They are the "altruists, those who make sacrifices; men are the egotists, those who make profits. Women are the conservers, the preservers; men are the despoilers, the destroyers."

He says that we've had enough of egotism and destruction in our world. It's time to give altruism, consideration for others and cooperation a chance. Society should give women a chance to make men more human than they are at the present.

How accomplish this? By entering business and politics? A French sociologist predicts that women will rule by the twenty-first century. Is this the answer?

EARLY TRAINING

"The most important job of a young woman today is raising good human beings." This may be inside or outside the home, or both. The best preparers of children are good mothers, and fathers who have had good mothers.

A Latin American friend of mine is appalled at our failure to train little girls to be girls. She thinks it's a serious mistake for them to play ball with boys when they should be playing house and dolls or learning to knit and cook.

According to Mr. Montague we should stop educating women in a masculine system, while hoping that somehow they'll remain women. Let's educate women, yes, but for the world of humanity which they are to help create. Even before girls enter school they should be educated in subjects related to womanhood.

EDUCATION A MISFIT

Phyllis McGinley, contemporary poetess, author and homemaker, laments the fact that society fails to recognize us as women. We are simply a different race, not a second-rate man. She lays part of the blame on our present educational system.

A woman's training is not tailored for her needs. Her education is a hand-me-down from man's shelf, an unaltered and misfitting garment. The American girl skips off to school and becomes a part of an enormous system, designed especially for boys. She's treated like a boy from kindergarten on through college. She studies the same subjects, becomes a sports enthusiast and expert, and is skilled in the same arts and professions.

She goes out from the coed world totally unprepared for her role, and in the process loses her feminine qualities.

No one has taught her that a woman chiefly needs "a terrible patience, a vast tolerance, forgiveness, forbearance, and almost divine willingness to forget private wants in the needs of the family"*

LOST RESPECT

Woman has won her freedom, but lost the respect of men. No longer do they hold the door open, nor give up their seats for her.

Joy Davies, a Toronto fashion commentator who operates a charm school for both men and women, expressed her views in a recent newspaper article. She says men will continue these traditional etiquette relationships if women remain feminine.

According to her, being feminine involves both "an attitude of gentleness, and kindness, and an appearance of good health, softness, neatness, poise and radiance."

She feels that since women are now in business, men have lost much respect for her. Too many career women have a hard shell. They swear, overdrink, oversmoke and are loud because they think this belongs to their new, more aggressive role.

---

*Phyllis McGinley, *The Province of the Heart* (New York: Viking Press, 1959).

Joy Davies concludes that women can be aggressive in a feminine way, with a gentle voice and manner that persuades rather than demands. In this way they will not lose the respect of men.

PSYCHOLOGICAL DIFFERENCES

Let's think a bit more about the differences in men and women.

By nature a woman is passive and receptive psychologically. Her basic traits are shaped by her primary need—to bear children and create a home for them. Her ego primarily is based on her performance as wife and mother.

Man is basically aggressive—mastering the world through intellect or physical bravery. His sense of accomplishment comes largely from his job.

Men and women are different sexually. Generally man is the aggressor, quickly responding to external stimuli. Sex is capable of giving a woman her greatest radiance. Marion Hillard points out that sex is "the force within her that makes her gentle with children . . . it's in the understanding she can give another human being who is lonely. She uses it, properly channeled, to enrich her life"†

A woman psychologist, Cleo Dawson, was asked to do some research on the differing psychological factors of men and women. She studied their different roles, and reports: Women basically feel while men

†Marion Hillard, "What Women Don't Know About Being Female," *Reader's Digest,* 409 (1956), 68:40.

think. Women frequently do surpass men in intelligence, but the weight of their emotional drag handicaps them. Men with their practical minds judge, organize and direct. "Nature's plan seems to be the supervision of woman by man," concludes Cleo Dawson. This coincides with God's verdict after sin entered the world, according to the biblical account (Gen. 3:16).

Men and women think differently, have different goals, enjoy different social activities, are physically different.

But can these differences be resolved by couples, outside of the divorce courts?

Indeed! They are intended to be complementary, not antagonistic. If man and woman could view their differences in this light, respect and cooperation would replace friction, hostility and competition. Then woman wouldn't want to "wear the pants," to be equal in the business, political and social worlds.

A woman must remember that the husband's qualities are necessary for her security, for the security of the children. A man must remember that woman's nature gives him the goals worth struggling for in life. These goals are love, a home and through children a psychological and biological immortality. The husband's highest aspirations are served by a wife's moral, emotional, social and sexual traits.

Woman is needed to give emotional security to our insecure world as she gives herself and her love to both husband and child.

MOTHER OF MANKIND

Woman's primary role and greatest contribution is that of being a mother. In an old magazine I ran across an article by Agnes E. Meyer. The principles still hold today. She pleads, "God protect us all from the efficient, go-getter business-woman whose feminine instincts have been completely sterilized. Wherever women are functioning, whether in the home or in a job, they must remember that their chief function as women is a capacity for warm and charitable human relationships."

Woman's humility—her ability to adjust to outward circumstances, to the husband in marriage, to the employer and fellow workers in business—is her strength. The weak woman tries to control situations by force, and by her outspoken aggressiveness.

The mature woman who knows her inner worth does not complain that she is unjustly treated, or denied high executive positions. She expands her area of influence.

She is not resentful of a man's role—not jealous of him because he doesn't get pregnant, stay at home and raise children, or do the housework. She realizes that men have a different and separate role!

"What the world needs today is not more competition, but woman's native genius for sympathetic cooperation—between public and private endeavor, between management and labor, between contending religious sects, between the family and the community, between one individual and another. This is woman's great opportunity—to ease the acute and dangerous tensions of American life," continues **Mrs. Meyer.**

This is largely accomplished in the home as a woman teaches her children true standards of conduct, and as she creates a refuge for her husband.

Agnes Meyer concludes that it's a great honor to be a woman in this critical period.

I'm reminded just now of Rose, a capable and talented woman who chose to remain feminine, to expand her area of influence through the lives of her husband and children, and not in the educational world. Her children were no menace to society, and today her two sons are influential missionaries; one daughter is married to a minister; three daughters are wives of successful Christian business and professional men. They in turn are mothers of happy, well-adjusted children. Her husband, through his ministry, helps hundreds. Could Rose have been as much an influence in society had she chosen to assert her equality with man? Or compete with man?

GOD'S DESIGN

God didn't create woman to be second-rate man!

After God had made man, He stepped back, observed him and then concluded, "He's imperfect. I must give him someone to complete him, to be his helper." So He made woman—loving, gentle, kind, understanding. Side by side they were to live and work—the woman not to expect too much feeling from the man, creating pressures and tensions; the man not expecting the woman to be too reasonable.

But together, the two would be one—cooperating, trusting each other's strengths, and allowing for weaknesses.

God purposely made woman a unique person to be helper to man—to be mother of mankind. This is her supreme role!

2

I PROMISE

I, Susan Brown, take thee, Robert Adams, to be my wedded husband, to have and to hold, from this time forward, for better or for worse, for richer or for poorer, in sickness and in health, to love, cherish, and to obey, till death do us part, according to God's holy ordinance; and thereto I give thee my troth.

AH, SWEET YOUNG BRIDE! Never has a bride been lovelier!

This is your day full of gladness and festivities—like weddings down through the ages. An account of a wedding in 1570 tells us that the bride, "her hair as yellow as gold, hanging down behind her" was led to church "between two sweet boys with bride's lace and rosemary tied about their silken sleeves."

Yes, your day with storybook charm.

On this your wedding day your mind naturally turns to all the blessed days ahead. A good marriage is a lifelong miracle. You and your husband truly cannot envision how blessed it will be! The poet Lyttelton wrote: "How much the wife is dearer than the bride."

17

"For better or for worse. Oh,
nothing can spoil our love!"

Nothing, my dear, absolutely nothing can spoil your love for the man by your side. If you don't let it.

This is a big order, what I'm about to tell you, but it is so true. God has placed in your hands the key to love. And from you, Robert will catch this love.

When he's laid off from his job, when the accident demolishes the car, when he's late for meals, when his plans conflict with your club plans—in these your love will understand, will comfort, will encourage without blaming, or criticizing, or continually questioning "why?"

Cheer him when he's depressed. Lighten his load whenever you can. Complain as little as possible. Look for a constructive approach to difficult situations. Make home a place where he wants to come.

It's a mystery, but God performs it when you take Him with you.

You need a triangular relationship. Not the triangle as depicted in today's society but a triangle formed by God, your husband and you.

"Two shall be one? How can this be?"
You *two* are now *one*.

During this first year you lay the foundation for the blending of two lives. So guard this first year well. "It counts most," says a noted marriage counselor. This is the year attitudes mature—when consideration for others, willingness to share, and the foundations of partnership develop. Any marriage, yes, even your marriage, is in danger until this is accomplished. This year counts most. Knowing this and putting forth all effort to make it count will insure the happiness only marriage can bring.

This calls for sharing, for confiding, for understanding, for frankness. "After love, being able to confide fully, freely, and frankly in each other is the most essential characteristic of a happy marriage," says the psychologist.

You are a woman—with a nature, a personality, distinct from man. You are feminine—sympathetic, understanding, kind, loving, with deep feelings.

He is a man. He reasons, manipulates and directs. Two distinct roles, two different personalities, so created by God your Maker. You are not competitive. Rather you complement each other. Man alone is incomplete. Woman alone is incomplete. Harmoniously blending, these two distinct personalities create one whole—a complete personality.

Take time to share each other's interests, plans, hopes and dreams. Take time to grow deep into each other's lives, to become one physically, mentally, emotionally, and spiritually.

> *"I wonder, can love be more wonderful than it is today?"*

Yes, Susan, love grows dearer and sweeter! Love understands and is kind. Love forgives and accepts forgiveness. Love sacrifices. Love is unselfish. Love gets up in time to become presentable and to prepare a nourishing breakfast before he leaves for the day. Love listens when he talks. Love shows sincere interest in his work, hobbies and recreation. Love plans for his rest and health. Love enjoys preparing nutritious meals, considering his likes and dislikes. Love pleases him. Love expresses itself verbally and in gestures, does not take him for granted. Love expresses appreciation and delights.

You must take time for physical love. This is the dessert God has prepared for a man and a woman, and reserved for marriage.

You see, love begins in the physical union, but tenderly cared for, nourished and cultivated, it spreads out into every area of your lives. Love is also fruitful—producing little ones, who become centers of combined, united interests and concerns.

> *"To love, to comfort, to honor,*
> *to cherish."*

Yes, Susan, that's what you can do best as a woman. These are your strengths. Woman is born to LOVE—in every form or expression.

You show love by loving. Love does not contradict. Oh, yes, love explains, may offer difference of opinions, but love seeks to arrive at the best solutions. Love proves what is right, not who is right.

Love speaks kindly. Angry words, condemnation or scorn will crush him. And when you take hope from the heart of man, you make him a beast of prey.

Comfort him when he's discouraged and everything goes wrong at work. Let him know he still has you, your love, a peaceful home, a shelter from life's adversities.

To honor him is important. Every husband needs a wife's acceptance, her admiration, her appreciation. When you recognize and fulfill Robert's ego needs, you are encouraging him to give his best to your marriage.

You can honor him as you: confide in him, thank him for little courtesies, show interest in his work, speak well of his relatives, compare him favorably with other men, humor his whims and quirks, respect his confidences, compliment his appearance, make his friends feel welcome, share at least one of his recreations, dress to please him, demonstrate your love to him, obey him and submit your will to his wishes at those times when you cannot agree.

Cherishing him makes him feel needed. Let him protect and care for you. A woman was created to receive. Allow him to give to you. Don't resist or turn a cold shoulder even to the smallest of his gifts.

"Till death shall part us."

Yes, Susan, till death separates you.

When you're tempted to trade him off for another, just remember that some adjustments with money, friends, personality differences, sex, and social interests may not be fully realized during the first few years. Some not for twenty. But stick to him. He's worth it.

You promised, "Forsaking all others . . . keep myself only for him." When your eyes are tempted to wander, pull the shutters. Just remember that any man has his faults when you live with him twenty-four hours a day.

The words of Jonathan Swift come rolling back across the years:

> "Let none but Him who rules the thunder
> Put this man and woman asunder."

Of course, true love doesn't guarantee the absence of problems. To the contrary, true love does have problems, but walks hand-in-hand through them.

Yes, no matter what happens. "Love never fails." And only your love, your faithfulness will cause him to want to do better.

Lose yourself in him. You won't lose your personality. Fulfillment does not come in selfish pursuits, in giving marriage and home second place. It comes in the philosophy of Jesus Christ: "Lose yourself for others, and you'll find life, but hold on to life [your identity] and you'll lose it."

Some say that freedom from domestic demands brings fulfillment. If so, then why has the modern wife *not* been fulfilled?

I share this letter from Gloria:

"I worked as a nurse until recently. Now I'm at home . . . and I can't forgive myself for not having done it sooner . . . Oh, yes, I miss contact with the girls, the 'shop talk,' the excitement, and appreciation from the patients . . . but I'm finding that the contented look on hubby's face as he steps in the door, his characteristic grin, his greeting and kiss, can be more rewarding . . . And the lack of tension and pressures created by my working schedule no longer exist. We have time for each other. I'm discovering who my husband really is. Honestly, I'm finding myself!"

Susan, you can't understand all I've tried to tell you. You can't and won't. But do remember what I said about the marital triangle. When you get in a jam, when you don't quite know what to do, quickly run to Jesus Christ. He can help you with anything. After all, He already knows it. Nothing, absolutely nothing is hid from His eternal gaze. Faith can lift you above anything and everything!

And when your day is bubbling over, when you've never been happier, tell Jesus about it. Yes, tell Him. Thank Him for giving Robert to you—and for the joys of marriage.

Dear bride, this is your day! God bless you!

3

HINTS FOR HOMEMAKERS

KEEP IN MIND the importance of your career as homemaker!

Your attitude toward your job makes all the difference in the world! It makes your day as palatable and enjoyable as a fluffy orange chiffon cake, or as distasteful as burnt toast!

Susie was tired of being referred to as a plain, everyday run-of-the-mill housewife. But she did consider that hers was the most important job she could be doing and that no one else could do it as well as she.

So she decided to call herself an artist. She says: "I am trying to raise children in this mad world and keep my husband happy. And if that's not art, I don't know what is!"

Soon after this bold resolve Susie filled out the papers to begin a charge account at the department store. She wrote ARTIST in the little space next to "wife's occupation."

The clerk who took the form looked at her with new respect. Susie left the store with such confidence and joy that she hurried home to create a new masterpiece for dessert. And she could hardly wait to take the hot iron and redesign the pile of crumpled clothes staring her in the face! The spell was marvelous! Her attitude about herself, her job had changed!

I think Susie's discovery would work for every woman who thinks that being a homemaker is a second-rate job, don't you?

CREATIVE

I've heard young homemakers protest, "I'm just stuck between these walls. I like to be creative!"

Frankly, no other job offers more creative areas than does homemaking.

There's home decorating. All of us engage in that to a greater or lesser degree. We refinish furniture, fix up the children's bedrooms, design and sew dresses and skirts. And what homemaker doesn't feel a surge of satisfaction as she views the glasses of transparent jelly she's just paraffined? Or the new salad? Her flower arrangements? Her plants? And how about the birthday and anniversary parties? Novelty cake decorating? We plant flower beds. Care for house plants. The list is almost endless. There's yet one more. How about the satisfaction and joy when together with your lover and God you fashion happy sons and daughters?

One pretty, happy young mother was the center of attraction as she "decorated her life with babies."

You have chosen to be a homemaker. Ask God, who designed you, to help you find joy and contentment in the creativity of your daily task.

ENJOY EACH TASK

Enjoy what you are doing *while you are doing it*. This resolve has transformed Carmen's life and her entire household. She was always thinking ahead —making the bed quickly so she could throw in the wash and get started to vacuum the living room. Now she enjoys each task as she does it. She enjoys smoothing the pillows, pulling straight the sheets.

Her life is filled with a tranquility she hadn't thought possible with four small children. Keeping house is no longer a *trap!* Because she creates an atmosphere of contentment and order, while enjoying the simple daily duties and finding pleasure in the things as she sees and does them!

ORGANIZE

My third hint for homemakers is: *learn to organize* your housekeeping chores.

Paul Popenoe, Director of the American Institute of Family Relations, says: "One of the problems (in an unsatisfactory marriage) may be as simple and as easily helped as disorganized housekeeping. . . . Surveys have concluded that poor housekeeping is a major factor in marriage troubles and that many homemakers could do their routine work in 40 percent less time than they now give to it—and do it better."

This was true in Lila's case. When she got help to make out a schedule for her routine housework and handle it more systematically she accomplished more with less effort. Then some of her other difficulties in her marriage relationship began to seem less important.

MOTIVATE YOURSELF

Maybe you think that you can't organize. Or that you need more equipment, more conveniences. Personally, I believe that you can organize and efficiently do your work with just what you have—if you have the motivation.

Recently I ran across an article for salesmen entitled *"Ways to Motivate Yourself."* It was so good, that with a bit of adaptation, I pass it on to you as a homemaker.

1. *Put your plans on paper.* Spell out your goals, as homemaker, and the ways to reach them. Be specific. What do you want to accomplish this week? Now break this down into daily tasks so that you have no excuse for not getting started. Check your list from day to day, and thereby check your progress. Hasty thinking and hasty working seldom accomplish much. They may even cost you more time. A job well planned is a job half done.

2. *Remind yourself of the benefits*: a happy husband, when he comes home to an orderly home and a satisfied, contented wife; calmer and more cooperative children—because Mom is calm.

3. *Avoid procrastination*—when it comes to the jobs that you know *have* to be done. It'll help to get an *early* start. Maybe you don't have to get up when hubby does, but try it. Prepare his breakfast, then take a calm thorough view of the day's load.

Spend a few early quiet moments reading the Bible and talking to God about your day's work. Then get started. Don't stall.

4. *Set deadlines.* Don't attempt more than you can do, but do determine to do what you can. Remind yourself of what'll happen if you don't have meals on time or if you don't have the shirts ironed. Set deadlines for some chores, but don't be glued to the clock. Be optimistic.

5. *Promise yourself rewards*—an hour of profitable reading, or knitting, or music or visiting next-door neighbor or sewing the new dress. Or an hour with your hobby.

6. *Give yourself the right to make a mistake.* No one's perfect, so exercise your sense of humor. Laughter covers over many a flub.

7. *Be flexible.* When the unexpected comes, and it will often, meet the interruption gracefully and positively. Then come back and take up the mop, or pans, or iron where you left off.

8. *Bring faith into the kitchen,* and into every room and household chore. Relax in Jesus Christ. Remember, He created you and is interested in every detail of today and every day. Do your tasks as serving God. Take time to read the Bible and to pray. Do it daily at a regular time, perhaps after breakfast as does Josephine Robertson:

AFTER BREAKFAST PRAYER

Dear Father, now that my family
has gone to work and to school,
a sudden quiet falls on this disordered house.

Help me to face the work for this day
    with a singing heart—
    the dishes to wash, the beds to make,
    the clothes to launder, and the picking up
    which sometimes seems as futile as
    sweeping a forest floor in time of falling leaves.
I thank Thee: that I am needed,
    that my job in these busy years
    is to create a home that will be a
    place of warmth and comfort and love.
Help me to see each task, not as a dull chore,
    but as a strand woven into a pattern of living.
Grant, I pray, that it may be a pattern to remember,
    a pattern of order, and beauty, and through
    it always may there gleam the golden thread
    of Christ's spirit.   —Amen.

SIMPLIFY HOUSEWORK

Now that you have the right attitudes toward the importance of homemaking, you have motivation, and you've asked God to help you, here are some *ways to simplify your housework.*

Find the way of doing the daily, the weekly and the seasonal chores that fits best into your family's pattern of life.

Plan your jobs so that you can stay on one floor of your home or in one area until you have completed them. This way you save yourself unnecessary steps. A table on wheels easily fixed by hubby can be used for assembling and transporting food, dishes, groceries, cleaning supplies, laundry and many other things from place to place. Keep all your cleaning supplies together in a basket.

Take a load off your feet by sitting to do any work you can, such as ironing, cleaning vegetables, feeding the baby.

When you sit to iron, place clothes to be ironed at your left and set a rack to hold ironed clothes at the right.

You spend a lot of time in the kitchen, so get organized there, too. Store seasonings, serving dishes and utensils needed at the stove right next to it and on easy-to-reach shelves. Utensils such as stirring spoons and pancake turners can be hung on the wall near the stove.

The height of your sink is important. If it is too low, place a rack in the sink underneath the dishpan to raise it to a more comfortable height. With thought and planning household tasks can be made easier and more enjoyable.

Whatever your hands find to do, do it with all your might (Eccles. 9:10). Do it the best way possible and enjoy it as you do it—knowing that an orderly, organized household gives you a better disposition, and adds to your husband and children's happiness.

A quote I clipped from a magazine years ago reads, "No woman does her housework with real joy unless she is in love."

Homemaker, enjoy your homemaking tasks—a tangible way of showing your love to the family.

4

A TRIBUTE TO MOTHERS

IT WAS A TYPICAL MORNING. Mother busily preparing breakfast. Father and the boys washing up after finishing the chores. Little daughter teasing and laughing. Suddenly all was quiet. But only for a moment. Then they all burst into the kitchen.

"Happy Mother's Day!" they chorused.

Father put his arms around Mother's shoulders as he presented the bouquet of roses. The children almost fought to be first with their individual tributes: a "homemade" greeting saying, "I love you, Mother"; a potted cactus; a paper scrawled with "Good for 5 car washes. This paper must accompany requests"; a lovely handkerchief. Each a tender token of the children's love.

Mother tearfully expressed her thanks. Then silently prayed, "Thank you, God, for the rewards of motherhood, and please, forgive my many failures!"

The tangible expressions of the family warm a mother's heart for many days.

My family isn't the demonstrative kind, so I especially treasure each sentiment of appreciation. As a mother of teen-agers, I was thrilled to hear last Mother's Day, "Thanks, Mom, for being *my* Mother."

MOTHER LOVE

Most beautiful things come by twos and threes, by dozens or hundreds. Plenty of roses, stars, rainbows, brothers and cousins. But only one mother in the whole world!

She may be called by various names—"Mom," "Marm," "Mamma," or "Mother," as is the case at our house. Each child has a pet term, all his own, but they all mean the same.

There come to my mind names of mothers of great men, such as Washington's mother; Lincoln's mother; and Mary, the mother of Christ. There is also the poor mother who scrubbed floors all day, and then gave blood in transfusions at night, to put her son through college.

A mother's love sacrifices. They say that even a mother spider lets her children devour her body, so that they may live by her death. She is courageous.

Joaquin Miller says:

The bravest battle that ever was fought,
   Shall I tell you where and when?
On the maps of the world you'll find it not,
   It is fought by the mothers of men.

Yes, mother hearts are same the world over. In all ages, in all lands, in all classes. Probably typical mothers of Hollywood or Las Vegas won't qualify. But it's like Mother to stand by, through thick or thin, through good or ill, through success or failure, when everyone else fails. Yes, Mother stands by to the end.

Rudyard Kipling says,

> If I were hanged on the highest hill,
>   Mother o' mine, O mother o' mine;
> I know whose love would follow me still,
>   Mother o' mine.

HANNAH — AN EXAMPLE

In thinking of a mother's heart, I recall Hannah (I Samuel 1). The Bible tells us that Hannah was one of several wives. This was customary for a man of those times. But Hannah was disgraced. She had no children. The other wife used this to ridicule her. Hannah was depressed. She could not be comforted, even though her husband suggested that he surely meant more to her than ten sons.

Hannah took the proper procedure. She talked the situation over with God. She prayed for a son. She went even further and promised that if God gave her a son she'd give him back to his Creator. In the course of time Samuel was born. Her joy was complete.

Hannah loved her child. She kept him close to her side. She rocked him gently to sleep. She played with him, and no doubt often repeated the story of his miraculous birth. She taught him about the great and powerful God.

Hannah was a woman of integrity. She kept her vow, and after weaning her son (probably from three to five years of age) she took him to live in the house of the Lord. What a courageous act! Of course, her mother heart was torn, but at the same time she was happy to give her treasure to God for His use.

Her mother love followed the child. Once a year she visited her son, probably spending several weeks with him. At this occasion she presented him a new garment woven by her own hands. Yes, woven not only with threads of wool or flax but with threads of love, of concern, and of prayers.

Hannah was rewarded. Her son became a famous prophet—one who knew God and who was loved and honored both by man and by God.

HER MOTHER HEART

Hannah is a challenging example as a mother!
She wanted her child.
She prayed for him—before and after birth.
She cared for him.
She loved him.
She taught him right living—the truths of God.
She returned him to God, his Creator.
She followed him with her loving care and concern
    all through the years.

Such mother love is a child's security. Throughout his entire life.

WITH MOTHER IS HOME

Just to be where mother is—that's home and rest.
"I wonder why," his auntie said,

"This little lad comes always here,
When there are many other homes
    As nice as this and quite as near?"
He stood a moment deep in thought,
    Then, with a love-light in his eye
He pointed where his mother sat
    And said, "She lives here, that's why."

A LITTLE PARABLE FOR MOTHERS
by Temple Bailey

The young Mother set her foot on the path of life.
"Is the way long?" she asked.

And her Guide said: "Yes, and the way is hard.
And you will be old before you reach the end of it.
But the end will be better than the beginning."

But the young Mother was happy, and she would
not believe that anything could be better than these
years. So she played with her children, gathered
flowers for them along the way and bathed with them
in the clear streams. The sun shone on them, life
was good and the young Mother cried, "Nothing will
ever be lovelier than this."

Then night came, and storm, and the path was
dark, and the children shook with fear and cold, and
the Mother drew them close and covered them with
her mantle, and the children said, "O Mother, we
are not afraid because you are near, and no harm
can come." And the Mother said, "This is better
than the brightness of day, for I have taught my
children courage."

The morning came, as they approached a hill. The
children climbed and grew weary. The Mother was

weary, but all the time she said to the children, "A little patience, and we are there." So the children climbed, and when they reached the top they said, "We could not have done it without you, Mother." And the Mother, when she lay down that night, looked up at the stars, and said: "This is a better day than the last, for my children have learned fortitude in the face of hardness. Yesterday I gave them courage. Today I have given them strength."

The next day came strange clouds which darkened the earth—clouds of war and hate and evil, and the children groped and stumbled, and the Mother said: "Look up. Lift up your eyes to the Light."

Then the children looked and saw above the clouds an everlasting Glory, and it guided them and brought them beyond the darkness. And that night the Mother said, "This is the best day of all, for I have shown my children God."

The days went on, and the weeks and the months and the years, and the Mother grew old. She was little and bent, but the children were tall and strong, and walked with courage. And when the way was hard, they helped their Mother; and when the way was rough, they lifted her, for she was as light as a feather; and at last they came to a hill from which they could see a shining road and golden gates flung wide.

And the Mother said: "I have reached the end of my journey. And now I know that the end is better than the beginning, for my children can walk alone, and their children after them."

Her children answered, "You will always walk with us, Mother, even when you have gone through the gates."

Then they stood and watched her as she went on alone, and the gates closed after her. And they said: "We cannot see her, but she is with us still. A Mother like ours is more than a memory. She is a living presence."

5

ENJOY COOKING

Do you enjoy cooking? Maybe you're thinking, "I would if my kitchen were an attractive place." I'd like to suggest that any kitchen can be attractive and enjoyable—if you make it so.

Maybe hanging onions on the wall might help. "What?" you question. "A string of onions make my kitchen pleasant?" Let me explain.

One mother became interested when her four-year-old daughter remarked that she loved to be in her girl friend's kitchen. Everything in it looked like a pretty picture. So on her next visit to the girl friend's home, this mother observed the kitchen. A cord of beautiful wine-colored onions hung artistically on a nail on the wall. A few yellow lemons in a pottery dish looked like a famous painting of still life.

These touches won't necessarily change the status of your kitchen in the eyes of others, but they can change your outlook and approach.

"Even an ideal kitchen, equipped with all the latest gadgets, arranged for maximum efficiency, won't quite run itself. It still requires a guiding hand and good management. Many things can be done in a kitchen, but the main business is preparing three meals a day.

"Dealing with food takes more hours each day and each week than any other household activity. There are two approaches. One is to hate it, resent it, and make short shrift of meals. The other way is to enjoy it, have fun at it, and create dreamy dishes to delight the family," says Mary Gillies.*

Cooking seems to be about the only creative job left in many homes. With the right viewpoint it can be an exciting adventure which will last a lifetime.

And to be a good cook you'll first need to realize its importance. Secondly, you'll need to study and observe; and lastly, you'll have to practice.

Someone has said, "Today when daughter gladly follows in the footsteps of mother they probably will lead away from the kitchen!"

I can't quite forget a cartoon which appeared in our daily newspaper. A man and wife were standing by a travel agency show window. The woman was gazing at the attractive airplane display. Underneath was written this caption, "Travel to strange, unknown places." The husband said to his wife, "May I suggest our kitchen, Dear?"

All this suggests today's trend—that more wives find cooking a drudgery instead of a pleasure.

---

*Mary Davis Gillies, *How to Keep House* (New York: Harper & Row, 1961).

WHY A DRUDGERY?

Why is cooking a drudgery? With today's lovely, attractive, step-saving kitchens and modern cooking methods, why has it lost its appeal?

I don't believe there's another country in the world where such a variety of good food is available as is here. And in contrast to other countries food is much easier to obtain and prepare.

My own experience in another culture verifies this! We had to prepare each day's meals from scratch! Daily we purchased our vegetables from one vendor, milk from another, fruit from still another, bread from the fourth one, and meat from a different cart. These all came to the door, we had to select the food, prepare it, then cook our meals on a charcoal burner or on a wood range. How differently here, where we buy packaged, nearly prepared, canned, frozen, or already baked food!

There certainly must be other factors involved, because it's not the lack of food nor unattractive kitchens that keep the homemaker out of her kitchen.

Some homemakers detest washing the dirty dishes that accompany cooking. I'm sure that even doing dishes would be a pleasure if homemakers had the attitude as expressed in this poem.

DIRTY DISHES

Thank God for dirty dishes,
  They have a tale to tell;

While others may go hungry,
   We're eating very well.
With Home, Health, and Happiness,
   I shouldn't want to fuss;
By the stack of evidence
   God's been very good to us.

Might it be that we feel cooking is a waste of time? The idea of cooking three meals daily? Twenty-one a week? Eighty-four a month? One thousand and eight meals a year?

Aren't we aware of their importance in a happy, successful marriage? Their importance towards building happy families? Many a man starts the day with preparing his own breakfast or eating at the coffee shop, while his wife lies in bed, fast asleep and unconcerned. How tragic! Maybe she doesn't have to get up as early as he, but she could go back to bed or snooze a while in the afternoon. A nourishing, warm breakfast prepared by a loving wife, plus a cheerful conversation during the meal, is the start every man needs for the day. Then, at the end of a strenuous day to be greeted by a contented wife and to find a nourishing, appetizing meal perfectly tops the day!

"The way to a man's heart is through his stomach." It surely is! Not that wife uses a delicious meal to "twist his finger"—to gain his "yes" to something he actually disapproves of. Oh, no! But the wife who's aware of her husband's need for good food already has his affection and interest. There's more to this; into such meals go much thought, love, and kindness. One grandmother advised her granddaughter, on her wedding day, to spend much time preparing her meals. She added, "You can't stir much love into a tin-can meal."

Let me emphasize, you are not wasting time when you prepare nourishing, adequate meals for your husband and children. Proper meals or the lack of them affects your children's health now, as well as in the future.

MOTHERS SHOULD TRAIN DAUGHTERS

It's appalling to hear of the number of young wives who were never taught to prepare three square meals daily! Others prepare meals from tin cans, from ready-mix boxes because they don't want to waste time. Still others don't want to be bothered, so they eat out. There's a tremendous pressure from the manufacturers of these foods and from the eating places. I was amazed to hear that a famous eastern restaurant has the slogan, "Let's take cooking out of the home." Why, to me, that's removing the core of the home!

I honestly believe that we mothers influence our daughters as to whether or not they'll enjoy cooking and washing dishes. We must have the right attitudes. We must take time to teach our daughters how to cook and bake.

Several years ago a young bride said to me, "I never cooked at home. Mom said I messed up the kitchen too much. She could do it better herself." Today that girl is separated from her husband. I'm wondering if not knowing how to cook might have been a determining factor in their separation.

The Bible commands the older women, mothers included, to be examples of the good life. We're to teach the younger women, our daughters, to be domestic. God intended that we mothers should pass on the torch of homemaking to our daughters. And this includes knowing how to cook. If we don't teach them, who will?

God knew that nourishing, adequate food was a vital part of happy family living. And preparing such meals contentedly and cheerfully is a source of pleasure and satisfaction for you, as homemaker. It goes a long way towards making your husband and children successful and happy.

Recently I noted this motto in a friend's kitchen, "Every girl should learn to cook, from her mother or from a book."

I'd say, preferably, it should be from her mother. However, if you didn't learn from your mother, don't use that as an excuse. Today many good cookbooks and magazines containing recipes and food articles are within your reach. I believe when you are aware of the importance of tasty, nourishing meals for your family, remembering that you are the key, then you'll put forth every possible effort, and even sacrifice, in order to become a good cook. You *can* enjoy cooking if you season the food with warm love.

6

A HEALTHFUL DIET

DAUGHTER JEANNE finally determined to lose a few excess pounds, and to the surprise of the entire family she stuck to her diet for two weeks. She absolutely refused to taste anything between meals. A decided contrast to her previous snacks between meals, and before going to bed at night. In fact, eating had been a favorite and enjoyable hobby! She even refused the tempting food her brothers poked in front of her nose.

However, the loss of the desired number of pounds was ample reward.

It seems society has put to scorn the well-rounded figure on the basis of aesthetic choice. Medical science disapproves of overweight on a health basis. Actors need to be ten pounds slimmer than normal for the sake of the camera. Clothing is styled for slenderness in the "right" places. Slim legs make the difference between acceptability or lifelong loneliness.

The jovial fat person is gone. Replaced by a slenderness which is difficult for the young person to maintain, or the older one to achieve.

So today we're caught between this concept of a

slim, beautiful body and an overabundance of food. People are looking for an answer. Hence the many diets and fads of weight control.

When I think of today's emphasis on health foods and diets, I'm really amazed at the many sickly youngsters in our land. Shouldn't they be healthier than those who lived fifty years ago?

ONCE UPON A TIME

In my parental home I recall the doctor's coming to our home only to deliver a child, and at my mother's fatal illness. We had childhood diseases, but mother had her own medicines and remedies. I myself first saw the interior of a doctor's office when twelve years of age.

Health and foods were never made an issue. Our diet consisted of ordinary foods—fresh vegetables from the garden, and all the watermelons we could eat in summer. Canned vegetables and fruit during the winter (and the peaches unpeeled). Turnips, carrots, potatoes and apples stored in the fruit cellar and used while they lasted during the fall. As much fresh milk as we could consume in drinking and in milk foods. All the fresh eggs we wanted.

Believe it or not, a favorite pastime as a child was to snitch soda crackers from the cupboard, run to the barn and dip them into the molasses barrel! No, we didn't eat the cow's grain, but we chewed fresh wheat kernels during harvesttime. It made tasty chewing gum. Our favorite morning cereal was cooked cracked wheat.

During the busy summer we ate meat once a day, but during the remaining months we might or might not have it daily. In the fall we stocked our pantry with hundred-pound sacks of dried beans, flour, rice, cornmeal and sugar. Then there were 5- to 10-pound pails of peanut butter, large boxes of dried fruit and of soda crackers, a case of canned salmon, and ten gallons of strained honey. I'll grant you, we didn't have a large variety of foods. We did, however, vary the preparation of the foods on hand. Snacks consisted of apples, or homemade bread or leftover pancakes with molasses.

UNDERNOURISHED TEEN-AGERS

It's quite a different story today.

A university doctor indicates that some young people have bad grades in school because of poor nutrition. Many children resort to candy bars, pastries and soft drinks for lunch. And bad eating habits can lead to physical and emotional problems, which impair scholastic performance.

A New Jersey survey of 9,000 high school juniors and seniors reports that four out of five eat poorly. Teen-age girls fared worse than the boys. Too diet conscious, they often avoided essential foods, such as milk and eggs. Many skipped breakfasts.

In other countries many teen-agers lack proper nutriment because of actual food shortage. But in abundant America it's tragic to know that boys and girls lay the groundwork for poor future health because they neglect to eat proper foods.

OBESITY AND HEART DISEASE

One forceful argument in favor of slenderness is that obesity supposedly is the major cause of heart disease. All right, now listen to this! In the little town of Roseto, Pennsylvania, the vast majority of the 1,676 residents are overweight, and yet heart attacks are almost unheard of there. The town doctor and undertaker moved out long ago. Their death rate is one third of the national figure. It's a tight-knit community composed of people of Italian descent. They eat great quantities of pasta and rich sauces, yet out of 388 overweight people examined by a medical team, only one showed evidence of heart disease.

However, this team did uncover some other interesting factors: there was little status-seeking or career tension. Most of the citizens had comfortable incomes. They were content with their lot. A happier atmosphere than found in most communities prevailed. People liked each other. Dr. Stewart Wolf comments, "We came away from Roseto convinced that overweight, even obesity, is not the single primary factor in heart disease."

Is it possible that our overconcern about diet and weight control produces the heart condition we strive to avoid?

WOMEN IN SOUTH AMERICA

I recall my impressions after living nearly seven years in a foreign land. Upon my return home I pitied the slender girls and women. I had grown ac-

customed to seeing the majority of the female popu-
lation pleasingly plump, and enjoying life! Their
facial appearance seemed more wholesome and
healthier. In contrast the American girls looked
sickly, appeared unhappier.

I recall one young senorita in South America
who had adopted the western idea of dieting. In contrast to her friends who hadn't accepted this fad,
she was very unattractive. The majority of the people, especially the men, pitied her, and didn't hesitate
to convey to her their sympathies!

I'm not ruling out all weight-reducing diets. Some
are advised by physicians. But, I've in mind this
prevailing idea that to be attractive and healthy one
must be slender. Maybe there are other things much
more important than weight for women and girls
to watch!

FADS AND FANCIES

A diet-conscious people can very easily go over-
board in their zeal and enthusiasm.

I'm aware that much of our refined, processed
and preserved foods are a far cry from those eaten
by uncivilized tribes, or even by our forefathers.
However, I do think it's a shame the extreme to
which this has gone. A sufficient quantity of organic
carrot juice is supposed to cure cancer, diabetes and
insanity!

Recently I read an article in which a doctor warns
people to use caution before accepting all these fan-
tastic ideas. He concludes that dozens of products

sold with health appeal profit no one but the salesman. And you should decide which come in this class.

Your body is a valuable possession. It is something you can never replace. You do want to take good care of it. You should be interested in including sufficient vitamins, and minerals found in fruits, vegetables, cheese, milk, and meat in your diet.

You should take care of your spiritual diet as well, for it is of great importance. Your body is called the dwelling place of God. And He needs a pure, clean place to live in. Your mind, ears and eyes should feed on those things which are pure, beautiful, honest, true and of good report.

Your spiritual body must be fed daily. Jesus said, "I am the bread of life." In order to be strong spiritually you must accept and know Him—His Word, His laws, His truths. You must digest them, let them nourish and strengthen every part of your life. You need faith in God to live a joyful life, free from tension.

Avoid crash diets too. You dare not go out fanatically on just one or two limbs of truth which Jesus gave. You need a balanced spiritual diet.

This is possible as you accept Christ in your life, as *you* read His Word and pray and commune with Him daily.

You need a healthful diet in order to have a healthy body. But more important is a proper diet in order to maintain a healthy spiritual body.

7

TRUE BEAUTY

WE CONSTANTLY are reminded of lily-white hands, soft-as-a-baby skin, a perfect complexion, aren't we? The magazines are full of attractive advertisements insinuating that your skin or complexion is the decisive factor as to whether or not you are accepted by others.

In order to sell their products cosmetic companies subtly teach a young girl that her Romeo will or will not propose, depending on her complexion.

I guess throughout history women have been interested in this subject. They've resorted to all kinds of artificial methods in an endeavor to produce the desired effect.

I was amused in reading that in 1770 British Parliament passed a law against women getting husbands by false pretenses. It reads as follows:

"That all women of whatever age, rank or profession, or degree, who shall, after this act, impose upon or seduce and betray into matrimony any of His Majesty's subjects, by virtue of scents, paints, or cosmetics, artificial teeth, false hair, Spanish Wool, iron stays, bolstered hips or high-heeled shoes, shall incur the penalty of the law now in force against witchcraft and like misdemeanors and the marriage under such circumstances shall be null and void."

Well, it's unthinkable that our Congress would pass a similar law today. But if it did, do you have any idea how many millions of dollars' worth of business would go down the drain? There'd be loss of advertising to papers, magazines, radio and television. Just think of the loss of jobs for the millions of workers in cosmetic factories, to say nothing of the income loss for the beauticians and the cosmetics industry. American women spend millions of dollars yearly on cosmetics.

All the fads around today that are intended to beautify women include more than aids for just the complexion. How about the hair dyes? I read that dye-it-yourself fans spend about 50 million dollars yearly on tinting products for home use! Terrific!

FACIAL SURGERY INADEQUATE

Some aren't satisfied with changing the color of their hair, with beautifying and softening their faces; they're even using cosmetic surgery to change their faces. Dr. Bernard Claove, one of France's leading plastic surgeons, reported that there has been a sharp increase in the number of European and American women who seek this method of beautifying themselves.

I was genuinely interested in this noted surgeon's comments. He said, "Most women seeking facial operations today are beautiful—but they want to be made more perfect. Their desire stems from a deeper dissatisfaction with themselves." This famous surgeon concludes, "A really happy person does not want to change her face, even if it is plain."

AN INNER FACE-LIFT

Dr. Maxwell Martz, leading New York surgeon, author and lecturer, says that while surgery can change the outward appearance of an individual, an inner or "spiritual" face-lift is necessary to remove old emotional scars.

In order to give yourself an emotional face-lift Dr. Martz gives some very important do-it-yourself concepts: Relax your negative tensions to prevent more scars from forming. Forgive others, for if you carry grudges, your looks and personality show it. Provide yourself with a tough (but not hard) epidermis instead of a shell. (You can't live creatively and fully if you are either too vulnerable or too enclosed in walls of self-protection.) And lastly practice a new and improved self-image to help you *feel and act* like the sort of person you want to be.

Dr. Martz adds, "The benefit of a 'new look' through cosmetic surgery can only be attained if a patient is satisfied with his or her 'inner look.' "

BEAUTY IS SKIN DEEP

Pseudo beauty is for sale everywhere; genuine beauty cannot be bought at any counter. Much of the craze for beauty focuses upon the folly of sham —to pretend to be what one is not to impress people. This causes life to become a meaningless masquerade.

People may be tempted to conform their standards to that of a paint slogan, "Save the surface and you save all." But this is not necessarily true. A thin coat of paint can cover a lot of rotting wood. Surface beauty only, in a piece of furniture or in a person, is repulsive. Most of us are interested in knowing if it is real. Beauty must attain inner soundness.

So—skin deep isn't deep enough. What's in your heart will come to the surface, regardless of facial surgery.

Today's commercial world has slyly caused women to believe that beauty is attained through excessive artificial makeup or a new face-lift. As though they're interested in your appearance and my appearance! If we only knew it—their interest primarily is in *what they get out of it.*

I don't know if lack of inner beauty of the heart necessitates all this artificiality, or if the easy access to these artificial methods has driven away an interest in the "inner look."

I'm thinking now of the old adages, "Beauty is only skin deep," and "Beauty is as beauty does." I'd like to add this one, "Beauty is as beauty thinks."

Dr. Martz's article confirms this, for he declares that your thoughts, ideas, ideals, and attitudes definitely affect your face, your beauty.

DIET AND HEALTHY COMPLEXION

I'm thinking of something else. What you eat very definitely affects your beauty. There's no doubt about it, but that the right kind of food helps to give a healthy glow to your skin.

I've observed young people who come from homes where proper foods have always been served. The foods weren't fancy or rich either, but they were nutritious. As young people leave home and begin frequenting the snack-shops and the lunch counters, they overbalance their diet with sweets, rich pastries, sodas, candy bars. Very soon, there is a definite change in their complexion.

DANIEL AND HIS FRIENDS

Remember the incident recorded in the Bible about four youths without blemish, handsome and skillful in all wisdom—Daniel and his three friends. They had been taken captive by the enemy and were being prepared along with others to serve the king. The king assigned to them "a daily portion of the rich food" which he ate and of the wine which he drank.

Well, Daniel and these other three fellows refused to be defiled with the king's rich food and wine.

Their caretaker was disturbed. He was under strict orders to give the young men the best. They finally persuaded him to consent to a ten-day test. They would go on a ten-day diet, eating the simple, yet nutritious foods they had eaten at home—lentils to eat and water to drink. At the end of ten days they would be compared with the others who ate the king's diet. There's no way of exactly knowing what "lentils" were but my guess would be it included all varieties of vegetables. They probably cooked them with a bit of meat as flavoring.

Well, at the end of ten days "it was seen that they were better in appearance . . . than all the youths who ate the king's food." If this experiment improved the appearance of these young men, it will probably do the same for girls.

TRUE BEAUTY OF THE HEART

Well, let's return to the effect of our emotions on our face, on our appearance. After observing many Americans on the streets one European visitor remarked that Americans were tense and unhappy. He could see it on their faces. You see, a heart full of sadness, of evil, of hate, disgust and grudges reflects itself on our faces.

In contrast, "A glad heart makes a cheerful countenance."

Mothers, let's emphasize true beauty of heart and mind and character. Let's remember that kind, gentle, pure, loving, happy and thankful thoughts, springing from a heart of love, create true beauty of face. We will not be loved primarily for our lily-white hands and school-girl complexion but for what we are— for what we think and do. Let's pass on to our daughters these beauty formulas which are guaranteed to give lasting results.

A thankful heart, like the one expressed in the following poem, improves one's complexion.

WHAT GOD HAS GIVEN ME

I haven't a mansion, title or wealth,
But I have my family, and good health.
I haven't a nickel on payday to spare,
To tell the truth, I really don't care.
I have the sun and the sky so blue,
And lots of good neighbors, too;
I have the stars and the moon so bright,
To light up the sky on the darkest night.
I haven't a yacht to sail on the sea,
But I have a husband that loves only me,
And so I thank God in heaven above,
For giving me these things to love.

VICKIE SCHUGG

You can become beautiful as you ask the Lord to remove your fears, your tensions, your grudges, your bitterness, your discontent and your sins. He'll replace these undesirable traits and emotions with His love, His kindness, His forgiveness, His joy, and His peace.

God knew from the beginning of time that the hidden beauty of the heart produces a beautiful face. He knew what the world-famed surgeons are saying today. He's ready to give you true beauty—if you want it.

8

YOUR DRESS SHOWS

WHEN MRS. JOHNSON moved into the nation's spotlight, Washington society writers frequently criticized the clothes she wore. After a year's time, one reporter wrote, "Even today she is no fashion plate." Why? They caught her wearing the same beige turban for months! And the same white chiffon evening gown!

But I personally admire Lady Bird's philosophy of clothes summed up in these words: "I like them pretty. But I want them to serve me, not me to serve them—to have an important, but not a consuming part in my life."

Queen Sirikit of Thailand, one of the world's greatest beauties, said, "I wear my dress several times. This also helps Thailand husbands. They tell their wives, "If the Queen can do this, so can you!"

Clothes serve these famous women. They are not slaves to clothes. Isn't this a sensible philosophy for any woman?

REVEALS CHARACTER

Someone has said, "The body is the shell of the soul, and dress the husk of that shell, but the husk often tells what the kernel is."

Philip Massinger, in the 16th century said, "As the index tells the contents of the book, and directs the particular chapter, even so do the outward habit and garments, in man or woman, give us a taste of the spirit, and point to the internal quality of the soul."

I got a jolt recently when I read a famous folk singer's remarks about his wife! He likes her with dirty, stringy hair and dirty clothes. Because dirt brings out the animal nature in one!

Well, he wasn't the first to discover that clothes have a moral effect upon people's conduct!

School authorities in several large cities have taken a firm position concerning dress. Simply because dress does affect the students' conduct.

Ninety-two Pittsburgh boys and girls in questionable attire were sent home from North Hills High School for a week. The principal said teachers had warned students and parents all year about outlandish dress and hair style.

The students were more polite, more courteous, more sensible when they wore decent clothing.

The board of education in Boone, Iowa, has tackled the matter of adopting a clothing and hair fashions code for high school students which includes: hair dyes are out; hair must be neat and orderly; a boy's hair shall not come below his ears.

Girls are not allowed to wear jeans, slacks or shorts in classes.

APPROPRIATE

It is important that people dress appropriately to the occasion.

I read in a newspaper that Bishop Vincent S. Waters, of the Roman Catholic Diocese in Raleigh, North Carolina, has announced rules of dress for all his churches and chapels. Because the church is God's house, and God "has an absolute right to our reverence." Waters says that "it would be unfitting for anyone, a member of a parish or a visitor, to be dressed in an unbecoming manner in the presence of our blessed Lord in church."

He further indicates that women are to wear traditional modest attire with sleeves and collars, proper necklines and backs. Women are not to appear in shorts, pedal pushers, jodhpurs, slacks, sunsuits, blue jeans, or any other contour-stressing clothes, which can become an "occasion of sin" to persons of the opposite sex. Women should appear in church as they would dress modestly for an audience with the pope, the president, or a king.

Men should not wear shorts or kilts or any garb except the traditional modest men's attire.

The same principle holds true in every situation —dress appropriately to the occasion, whether at church or at the beach.

PROMOTE DECENCY

It's satisfying to me to note that people still exist with a sense of decency and modesty. I was pleased to read of the Dallas group who sponsor *"Miss Teenage America."* Unlike ordinary beauty contestants, these girls make no appearances in bathing suits. Their measurements are not part of contest records! Judges select the queen on the basis of personality, talent, charm and awareness of local, national, and international events!

Hurrah for the sponsors, Teen America Association, Inc., who "emphasize the good, productive, decent, intelligent aspects of most of our nation's young people!"

Big-company executives also have their views. A survey conducted in Chicago has isolated the ten most frequent reasons why girls don't get jobs. One you might never have thought of: Hair bows. According to the study, the hair bows are a typical affectation among girls who have an immature attitude. So are casual shoes, sausage curls and giggling.

INDECENCY

Several years ago Carol Channing said, "I know there are women haters in the world. But why do they have to design women's clothes for a living?"

However, I hasten to say there are many clothes designed today that are very becoming, neat, and decent. I personally react to the tight, revealing lines—pants, shorts, sheerness, and near-nudity—as being immodest when they appear in public.

Dealers and designers recently introduced nude styles, thinking that probably they would be accepted in five or ten years! But people wanted them now! "And nobody is more surprised than the designers who brought it about and some of the buyers who are buying it," wrote a news reporter.

CONFUSION

Why do people accept such indecency?

Recently addressing a church group, marriage counselor Dr. David R. Mace explained: "Our whole culture is involved in a serious confusion between femininity and sexuality. American men, feeling that there is a lack of femininity in their women, are demanding that they dress and behave in a more sexually provocative way.

"But this is really an adolescent misconception of what femininity is. The erotically aggressive woman is often the very opposite of femininity, because what she is doing is to try to compensate for her inward lack of femininity by putting on a big show on the outside. The femininity of the kind that attracts a mature man is marked by a shy, modest sweetness, rather than sexual aggressiveness.

"However, American women are clutching desperately at straws. So now, with the help of fashion designers and cosmetics manufacturers, they are going all out to parade their erotic qualities. Lips, busts, and legs are prominently displayed, in a pathetic attempt to regain outwardly what they have somehow lost inwardly."

A REAL LADY

The Scriptures tell us older women are to be examples of that which is right. And I believe God expects us mothers to train our girls to be feminine. And it begins with babyhood.

Many women are really not aware of what's happening. Some are. Dorothy's 8-year-old son bragged about his playmate's mother, "She's a real lady, Mom. She wears skirts all the time." This was the same little boy who at three years of age had told her to put her dress on again when she appeared in a pair of black slims that she thought were sharp!

This mother admits that wearing skirts does have something to do with being a lady! And if women expect men to show them little courtesies, they should not dress and act like men.

Her friend's five-year-old daughter wanted to wear jeans—even to Sunday school and parties. So the mother switched to "wearing skirts full time herself. . . . This little girl rediscovered the joy of dressing up to look sweet and adorable, as a little girl should."

After thinking carefully, Dorothy is looking around for a comfortable cotton dress. She says, "I would be very pleased to have my son think of me as a real lady."

Samuel J. Cohen, manufacturer of girls' clothes, thinks that fathers should come home in the evening to be greeted by glamour girls, not tomboys. "But," he asks, "if Mom is wearing slacks and little Mary wears shorts, where's the glamour?" Mr. Cohen continues, "It's pathetic when a woman forgets the art of womanhood. That's the thing that attracts and holds a man. He can get his meals in a restaurant and have his socks washed at the laundry. What he comes home for is to enjoy feminine beauty and companionship."

Mr. Cohen's small granddaughter wanted to put on her party dress and patent leather pumps when she got up one morning. But her mother took the party clothes firmly away and laid out overalls and play shoes.

Then the small daughter went back to bed, remarking, "I guess it's just not worthwhile getting up today."

SIMPLICITY AND DECENCY

The feminine woman dresses simply, decently and modestly, not in fashion's extremes.

A. B. Simpson says that the truest dress is controlled by simplicity and decency so the observer fails to remember anything special and the wearer forgets about her dress.

"Nothing so well becomes true feminine beauty as simplicity," says G. D. Prentice. "Virtue is the greatest ornament, and good sense the best equipage," is G. Seville's comment.

Your dress shows your true self! The Holy Scripture advises woman's clothes to be decent, modest, inexpensive. Her adornment that of the inward beauty—a gentle and quiet spirit. Her hair styled neatly, not outlandishly. For a woman's beauty and attractiveness does not consist in artificiality, in expensive outfits, in latest hair fashion, in exposing her body.

Your dress can never hide your character. You are more important than your clothing. Beauty must be in you. Simple and well-chosen dress enhances that inner beauty.

9

HOMEMAKERS SHARE

DO YOU RECALL the newspaper account of the "mystery boy"?

The entire country was stirred, shocked, and maybe even angered. Policemen found the abandoned child at Miami International Airport. He was glassy-eyed, in a state of apparent apathy, with not one bit of identification. The labels in his stylish shirt, trousers, and shoes were efficiently removed, and he had only three cents in his pockets!

Later, as the officers located his parents and pieced the story together, hearts rose in sympathy with the bewildered mother who had deliberately abandoned her son. I felt sorry for her. She had a problem that was too big for her. And maybe she had no one to turn to, no one to confide in. And so she finally solved it in her own way.

Perhaps she was far from her family and friends —away from those who understood her situation, and cared. Maybe she was all alone in a strange town, hesitant to mix with others because of her child.

Maybe her husband was away most of the day occupied with his business and interests.

At least, this is how I envisioned the situation.

NEED TO SHARE

Would a homemakers fellowship have helped her find a better solution?

Mothers need times of talking-it-over, of exchanging ideas, of sharing common problems and concerns, of discussing new situations as well as comparing the joys and rewards of motherhood. We're just made that way!

In other years there were probably two women to a household—mother and grandmother, or widowed aunt, or maiden sister. The women worked together —conversing, sharing, solving in their normal daily conversation. Mother was freer to be a wife, to lavish time, love and praise upon her husband. Freer to comfort, to show concern, to show love to each child. She had time to think through situations. The moral support, maybe even the silent help, of just another woman's understanding presence boosted her morale, encouraged her and strengthened her. She found a release before she bottled up the new and difficult daily experiences of caring for a husband and children.

In other lands women gathered together almost daily at the village well. As they drew the water into their jars they chatted and shared together. Then they walked back home carrying a burden on their heads, not on their hearts.

Maybe in America the modern laundromat, in a measure, furnishes this time of fellowship, of sharing by a group of women who are bonded together in the common occupation of homemaking.

Marie eagerly anticipates the semiweekly trek to the nearby laundromat. She packs clothes, detergent, Suzy and Billy into the back seat with the laundry, and drives to the laundromat.

While the clothes are swishing Marie gaily chats with Esther and Jane. They plan doing their laundry together just so they can visit.

What I'm trying to say is just this: In every age and in every culture women need each other to share, to comfort, to encourage, to help, to care. And if this is lacking there are serious consequences, affecting not only the woman herself, but her home, her husband, each child—and consequently her community and church. Put these homes and communities and churches all together and you have a nation.

REWARDS OF SHARING

Sharing makes us more understanding of the problems involved. Ann insisted that her six-year-old son, Joey, was just plain naughty. He wouldn't obey her command to walk, not run; to sit still at the table, not dangle his feet against the rung of the chair; to sit quietly for the entire hour in church. Joey deliberately rebelled, she thought. Strained relationships, sharp criticism, lack of appreciation, and wrong attitudes began building up in her mind. Molehills became mountains.

Then one day Priscilla dropped in for a visit. In the course of their conversation Ann mentioned Joey's rebellion. Priscilla listened wide-eyed. Then she mentioned that was exactly how she had felt until she read that one of the needs of a six-year-old is exercise, almost constant movement.

That completely changed Ann's attitudes toward Joey. Slowly a warm relationship developed as Ann quit accusing him and learned to accept him and his need for activity. She encouraged strenuous outdoor activities to eliminate running in the house.

Another woman thought her husband was the only one who so often forgot his car keys and had to run back for them—until she joined a homemakers fellowship and heard Ruth laugh about this same trait in her husband.

Sharing relieves the homemaker's mind when she realizes her problems and concerns are typical ones and not the unusual.

Sharing reveals workable solutions as she listens to another's "how-I-solved-it."

Sharing brings release as she unloads and airs some concerns.

Sharing strengthens each person in her new resolves.

PRAY TOGETHER

Not only do homemakers share and solve and strengthen each other but those who know God pray together. To pray over their problems binds them together. They pray asking for wisdom from God who is the Source of wisdom. They pray to the One who promises, *"Ask,* and it shall be given you; *seek,* and you shall find; *knock,* and it shall be opened unto you" (Matt. 7:7).

Together they *ask* for guidance, *seek* for solutions, and *knock* at God's heart wanting more wisdom, more love and goodness, more faith, self-control, gentleness, kindness, understanding, and mercy. These God is qualified to give and does give generously and willingly.

HEART TO HEART CLUBS

Several years ago I encouraged homemakers to form fellowship groups. We called it a *Heart to Heart Club.* (Now called *Heart to Heart Fellowship.*)

I've been delighted with the many letters coming to me telling of the various groups formed. Some meet weekly, for a brief period during the day. Others meet for a longer period at night. Others meet monthly, or every two weeks, whichever fits best into their schedules. Some are newly married girls, some young mothers, some are mixtures of all ages. One is an elderly ladies group. Another consists of a mother, her married daughters and daughters-in-law.

One group combines sharing and service: "We are enjoying our Heart to Heart Club immensely. Getting together and talking things over has been a great help to all of us. The last several meetings we have been embroidering pillowcases during the discussion period."

Another club reports rapid growth: "I'm thrilled with our club. In fact, we've grown so much that we have decided to break up into three smaller groups who meet weekly. Then once a month we meet all together."

Another group is happy to "have found a closeness and the freedom to share problems with each other we haven't been able to find in any other meeting."

A pastor has cooperated and given one group every third and fifth Sunday afternoon at the church. They eagerly look forward to these times for the Lord is "blessing them graciously."

Several groups report inviting new neighbors and unsaved mothers into their fellowships, as together they share in a common cause.

I received one letter from a mother in the hospital at the birth of her fourth child. She said, "How I do enjoy and appreciate our Heart to Heart Club. We've grown so much closer to God and to each other because of it. Two of my 'Heart to Heart' sisters are helping my three older children while I'm away. Thank God for those who care!"

This is indeed encouraging! I thank God that these many homemakers are finding a new joy and contentment in their everyday tasks.

I find many women had great ambitions in their younger days. Maybe they even prepared for a career or committed themselves to a special work for the Lord. Then they married. And in the pressure of day-by-day living and coping with the different personalities of a family they became defeated, discouraged, even bitter. They feel they have missed their calling. A sharing group helps homemakers regain a sense of purpose, a higher evaluation of their tasks, and a loyalty to their day by day responsibilities and privileges.

Many homemakers tell me they and the atmosphere in the home have been completely changed since they have become aware of the importance of their career. They find that doing the everyday tasks is God's will for them!

Yes, accepting God's will, and sharing with each other, does bring new courage and solutions and joy to homemakers.

Would the helpless boy have been abandoned in Miami if there had been a homemakers fellowship—to share—to care—and to help bear his mother's load?

I wonder.

10

WORKING MOTHERS LOSE

SOME MOTHERS WORK because of necessity. They have no choice. Other mothers take a job as the road to more freedom. Some seek self-fulfillment. But the majority simply want more money.

Sixty-two percent of mothers working outside the home say they want additional income or money for extras.

I cannot introduce the commandment, "Thou shalt not work outside thy home." That would be ridiculous! Mothers need to work. In the past they worked long, hard hours! Women worked in the small shop or on the farm. A mother worked alongside of husband and children. She was available. She could stop weeding the garden or leave the shop if her child needed her. Also her work was directly related to the family, and to their needs.

TIMES HAVE CHANGED

But today's work is vastly different. It's away from home, away from husband (and usually with someone else's husband). And when wife fails to provide love and companionship, many husbands find it elsewhere.

Mother's work is away from children. There's a constant shift of babysitters. There's no continuity in the child's life, no mother's love and tenderness when he is ill or in trouble. These conditions create deep and tragic problems for today's families. And I think mothers should be aware of them before taking on a job. They may find something to do at home that would bring an income.

Of the twenty-three million working women, there are eight million mothers with children under eighteen and three million have children under six. These mothers are contributing to our advanced civilization, to our materialistic living. But they are paying a great price. They personally are the losers.

IDENTIFICATION

What does a working mother lose? Probably foremost is identification with her child.

Dr. Habib Nathan, a University of Florida psychiatrist, conducted a research concerning the results when mother is separated from her preschool child.

He found that the "most outstanding result was the high incidence on antisocial tendencies—lying, stealing, no sense of right and wrong, destructiveness and absence of guilt," as well as a greater preoccupation with their own bodies. These children also showed less identification with parents.

His studies revealed that "the separation anxiety

that a child attached to his mother experiences daily, is equivalent to a discontinuity of relation."

You cannot be away and at home at the same time. Being away too much gives the child the impression that he doesn't count.

MONEY

A working mother loses money. "Working wives lose more than they gain," concluded a research report published by the Department of Agriculture. They work mostly for the extras—extra car, TV, kitchen appliances, advantages for the children. But how about the actual take-home pay? Deduct the extra clothing, food, transportation costs, child care, Social Security taxes, federal and state income taxes and what's left? One man figured that his wife earning 250 dollars monthly would have a net earning of less than 50 dollars. Is that sum enough to justify the extra pressures? Besides, her services may be more valuable at home.

Some estimate that the value of the average home-maker's contribution to the home and family ranges from $3000 to $7000 yearly.

COMPANIONSHIP

A working mother loses the opportunity to establish warm, understanding companionship.

Jane has no spare time. She comes home tired, too tense to do her work at night. As her own mother said, "She works all day and screams at the children all night!" So, Jane tries to make up for it by giving

Johnny a new bike, Mary a new outfit of clothes, and her husband a movie camera. Yet her children, especially her daughter, should be watching her, helping her, and learning important lessons. This is part of their education.

PEACE OF MIND

A working mother loses peace of mind. She has little time for her family. She isn't empty enough. Her mind's too preoccupied with her job, her work problems, her responsibilities away from home.

So she feels guilty. Especially when it's time to rush to work—Cathy is crying because she hates nursery school, Johnny has a sore throat, and the babysitter calls to say that she can't come.

TEACHING AND SHARING

A working mother loses the opportunity of sharing with her children, of teaching them.

Rosemary Rogers says, "Children don't develop character on a schedule. Day after busy day, lunch time with my three children under seven consists of little more than, 'Stop kicking the table, dear,' 'Yes, you have to eat your carrots,' and 'For goodness' sake, stop putting spaghetti in your hair!'

"But then one day, while I'm washing jelly off the wall, comes a question so basic that it challenges my keenest judgment to give the right answer. 'Mama, what does it mean to get married?' 'Mother, what is God like?' 'Mother, why is it wrong to tell lies?' When these important questions arise unexpectedly out of the bedlam, I want to *be there*. If these basic questions receive wrong answers, or no answers at all, they may never be asked again. If I miss my chance, this particular opportunity to help mold my child's character and his future happiness may be forever lost."*

WORK IS ESCAPISM

But mothers continue to argue, "I have to get away. Then I can love my family better!" Others seek only self-fulfillment.

I believe either approach is purely a selfish one. Such a mother thinks only of herself! Not of her husband and child, now, in the future or through all eternity!

What disturbs me is that even doctors advise mothers to get away! Why don't authorities help a mother to adjust, to learn the skills she needs and to develop right attitudes, rather than to encourage escapism?

REWARDS OF MOTHERHOOD

Mrs. Rogers, who has a science teacher's license, continues: "Sometimes I think longingly of a spotless office, sensible adult conversation, more pretty clothes, more spending money, more recognition for my talents. Sometimes I too ask myself, 'Is it really worth all this?'

"But my doubts vanish like drops of water on a

---

*Rosemary Rogers, "Weekends Aren't Enough," Used by permission.

hot griddle when my older son bursts in and says, 'When I get big, I'm going to be a scientist and find out if there are really any people on Mars!' And I am a millionaire when my four-year-old daughter beams lovingly at me and says, 'When I grow up, I'm going to be a mama!' "†

Cake mixes and dirty diapers do not constitute motherhood for her. Not "just anyone" can dry her children's tears, kiss the hurts, answer the questions and help in the shaping of her children's attitudes as well as she can. Furthermore, she has no regrets for being educated. "There is no more valuable use for any amount of education than full-time motherhood . . . and through this background I have been able to give my children intelligent answers to hundreds of questions about space ships, germs, electricity, caterpillars, flowers, their own bodies. . . . We explore the woods together by day, gaze at the stars at night. And through it all their little minds learn reverence for the Almighty God who created all these wonders."‡

Jessie Bernard, sociologist at Penn State, made a study of faculty women. She does "not believe that their contribution as academic women is necessarily any better or more socially useful in every case than their contribution as wives, mothers and community leaders."

---

†*Ibid.*
‡*Ibid.*

WHAT CAN BE DONE?

I think we as a nation should adjust our new patterns of work to motherhood. As Dr. Bruno Bettleheim, professor of education at the University of Chicago, suggests, "We must try to make arrangements so that a mother's work can again be of such a nature that she can still be available to her children as the need arises"—before and after school, and in cases of emergency.

He also advises that the adults caring for the young child "must not only be permanent figures in his life, but ones who will consistently provide meaningful and satisfying experiences to the youngster, which are also in accord with those his mother provides."§

COUNT THE COST

A working mother with her husband must realistically count the cost. The eternal values of life dare not be lost! They need faith. God has promised to supply the necessities of life if we obey His words. "Seek ye first the kingdom of God, and his righteousness; and *all these* things will be added unto you" (Matt. 6:33).

The Bible also says women should by example teach daughters to love their husbands and children, to be domestic, to be pure, kind and submissive to husbands, and in so doing teach God's ideas of life. This requires mother's presence, her constant love, concern and understanding.

I believe this is still God's idea for mothers.

§Bruno Bettelheim (ed.), "Why Working Mothers Feel Guilty," *Redbook* 126:55ff. (March, 1966).

As homemakers cultivate an appreciation for their vocation of homemaking, as they keep in mind the tremendously rewarding sense of fulfillment in the privilege of creating and nurturing the most precious of God's creation—a living soul—an outside job will not be so tempting.

Rosemary Rogers pleads, "Think twice, mother, before you rush out to that tempting career in the big, glamorous world. You have a vital career waiting for you at home. Your children's biographies are waiting to be written [tense nights], and weekends aren't enough!"

11

THEY NEVER MARRIED

I WANT TO PAY TRIBUTE to some of the many unmarried women who have contributed to my life, making it richer, more meaningful.

ELLA

I begin with Ella, my first Sunday school teacher whom I remember. She invited us as preschoolers into her home for Sunday dinner—probably one of those first occasions away from home, without parental control. Another time she supervised us in writing letters to our Sunday school paper. Through it I found a pen pal, with whom I corresponded for nearly twenty years.

Throughout my growing years in my home community Ella was there. And later, after my husband and I were on the mission field, Ella sent us a big scrapbook featuring photos of every family in my home church. It was such a thoughtful gesture! Although I tried to tell her, she can never know just what that meant to me—8,000 miles away from home and loved ones—as I pored over those pictures. I reminisced. I relived many experiences, and recalled many happy occasions with those who were a part of my earlier life.

That scrapbook was a result of much thought, effort and time as Ella got the families together, snapped those dozens of photos, developed them, then carefully assembled them in the book.

RENA

Then I think of Rena, a jolly, vibrant and enthusiastic woman, full of new ideas and ventures. Rena projected herself, in a positive, constructive way, in our youth activities. We young people felt something was missing if she was absent at our gatherings. In those days we didn't practice segregation of ages. Old and young mixed with each other. And anyone who felt young was welcome in our youth group! If I remember correctly, it was she who gave the ideas, even initiating some of them, for our youth organization. That was over thirty years ago when we had our socials, service projects, literary programs, spiritual meetings.

We sang for shut-ins in our community, also at the county home and at church. Come winter, we furnished stove wood for several elderly couples, for a widow, and for three maiden sisters—one a cripple. I say "we"—really the boys cut the wood, and we girls cooked and served the meals.

Rena was an inspiration, and added spark to the activities. She belonged to us. Although Rena married later in life, I remember her as a single girl.

LOIS

In later life, there were the maiden teachers—Miss Miller, Miss Good, Miss Wyse, Miss Rohrer—who always challenged me. But I must make special mention of Miss Winey, Lois, who opened up her heart and home to a needy girl. I lived with her one year as a college student. She taught me much about the economics of running a home. She counseled and encouraged me in the choice of a boy friend. And, I accepted her good counsel. I married the one she recommended!

And her interest didn't stop there. She helped with our wedding plans, served the wedding breakfast and helped me as no one else could on that joyful day.

UNA AND MABEL

I must hasten on. There are Una and Mabel, missionary nurses, who were close to me and my family in our stay among the isolated and illiterate Toba Indians in northern Argentina. During several months of hospitalization, Una often helped care for three motherless boys at home while Mabel came almost daily to my bed to give a back rub, fix me eggnog or do something for the new baby girl.

OTHERS

And now today there are Mary, Milly, Shirley, Nancy, Olive, Dorothy, Grace, Lovina (to name only a few) who are contributing to my life.

For all these, and many others I have forgotten or

can't take time to mention, I wish to express my appreciation.

Recently, Lovina walked into my office and enthusiastically reported about her Sunday school class of children, 10- to 12-year-olds, about entertaining the college girls, confined to dormitory life, about her contacts with little children through baby-sitting. Her final words were, "Tell you, I'm not bored with life!"

There are many Lovinas—enjoying life, busy in service for others, and for God.

But there are many who are not enjoying life. They're critical, complaining, harsh and demanding. What makes the difference?

I'd like to propose some reasons that make the difference. You think that I don't know because I never was a maiden lady? You might be surprised. I didn't marry until I was 26!

ACCEPT LIFE

Basic, and foremost, the unmarried woman must accept the truth. The one who always looks over the fence thinking that pastures are greener there will never be happy. That's true for any one of us women, married or single! Happiness comes in living above disappointments and not becoming bitter.

If you belong to the single girls, accept the fact— as God's will for you. Then, and only then, have you started on the road to contentment and peace.

As Betty Elliot, the martyred missionary's wife, says, "Only in acceptance lies peace, not in forgetting, not in resignation, nor in busy-ness. His will is good and acceptable, and perfect!"

FIND GOD'S PLACE

Next, find your place in life. With your personality, with your individual talents (or talent), with your abilities, what niche does God have cut out for you?

The local church, the hospitals, missions, institutions, old-people's homes, rest homes, orphanages, schools, the professional world—these and many other areas need the unmarried woman. You often can accomplish more than a married woman since you are free to come and go, not limited by home and family duties.

FIND A HOBBY AND FRIENDS

Next take up an interesting, challenging hobby. You need something to fill in when you're off work. If not, you can easily become bitter with self-pity, jealousy and loneliness. Also cultivate many friendships.

Acquaint yourself with an aged couple, if you do not have the love and interest of your own parents. Or enter deeply into the lives of nieces and nephews. If they aren't close by, find someone else. Like Lovina does. Her nieces and nephews are far away, so she exercises her "mother love" through baby-sitting, and her class of youngsters at church. Maybe there's a child, or children, nearby needing love and kindness. Follow them in their daily ventures. Remember them on special occasions, as Christmas and birthdays.

Katherine says in her letter to me:

I am a retired teacher of great age. I have always loved children and still do. I have spent most of my life in their company and service. I helped my brothers and sisters bring up a dozen. When I was past 65 years of age, my brother and I took two little homeless girls into our home. Now they are grown and married. One of them and her husband live with me now so I will not be alone. The other one has two beautiful little girls, two and four years of age. They come to see me often. Although I have never been a mother, children have given me the greatest pleasure and satisfaction of my life.

LIVE WITH SOMEONE

Live with others. Never live alone. Share your apartment with another girl or perhaps rent quarters in a home where there is some sharing with a family.

Maybe buy a home, and invite several other single women as paying guests. You need someone with whom you can share interests, joys and sorrows, ideas and problems.

Naturally, there'll be more adjustments than in living alone, but this helps keep you approachable, helps give you a more normal pattern of living.

Take the initiative in forming new friendships, in entering into the community and church activities. In the church you'll find those who care. Singleness often breeds selfishness. But before preoccupation with self becomes too ingrained, you must learn to share and identify with others.

FACE SEX

The single girl must also honestly face her sex life. Don't kid yourself with today's solution as projected in current books and magazines, or promoted by the doctor who told a group of student nurses, "If you don't get married, at least have an affair." If you're frustrated now, let me tell you, you'll be more frustrated after an affair! And one often leads to another, and another. God condemns sexual relationship outside of the marriage union. Sin is still sin.

In times of great temptation and loneliness, get close to God, ask Him to help you through the temptation. Then help Him answer your prayer by losing yourself in a worthy effort—creative writing, sewing, painting, playing the organ, visiting a needy friend.

I think it will also help you to maintain normal wholesome friendships with men of your acquaintance—a brother, a brother-in-law, a cousin or a close family friend.

ONE DAY AT A TIME

You can't foresee the future, but you can *accept* God's will for you now. You can give yourself to worthwhile work and activities of love. You can live one day at a time, and turn your life over to Jesus Christ's control—to find joy and contentment.

Who knows, but that sometime in the future there will be a man who needs you to complete his life and home? If not, you will have no regrets.

12

NOT ALONE

I SAW HER SITTING in the crowd, only a week after losing her husband. With her were five-year-old Jackie and twelve-year-old Susan. Sixteen-year-old Bob was with his friends.

No swollen red eyes, no drooping lips disfigured her face.

But I knew death's sharp knife had cut a deep wound in her heart. Moments later my few awkward words sounded hollow. They seemed to bounce back at me.

She smiled, "Thank you, Ella May. I'm so glad you came over to me. I thought I couldn't come today, but I might as well face reality. I can't stay at home forever." Then she glanced at Jackie, "I want the children to live as normal a life as possible."

We talked a bit about the comforting hope of once again meeting her husband in heaven, about his readiness to leave the pain-racked body behind.

LONELINESS

"A widow's life is a very lonely life," wrote Jane. No one can deny that! Loneliness follows the widow as sure as her shadow. One day you talk, laugh, plan, discuss, and pray with the partner of your heart. The next day he's gone. This only brings a void, a lonely spot in your heart and home.

Alone you attend the church and community activities. You feel like an intruder at social functions. But worst of all is nighttime. The work's all done. It's dark. The children are in bed, and you are alone.

One wife told me she found herself hurrying many times to share a bit of news, or the arrival of the cardinals, or the sunset's glow. Only to stop suddenly and remember husband was no longer there.

Susie wrote me, "Lately I've been blue, and felt that for all the things I've done there's hardly been a thank you. Now I must admit I have not actually been grateful enough for God's mercy—being a young widow trying to maintain my husband's business, I have much to thank God for, yet I've felt so lonely at times."

I think this introduces another important point: *resignation*. And, of course, contentment and gratitude. The widow who all her remaining days complains or questions "why" or envies others or feels God "picks" on her—this woman lives a lonely, hard life. But as she from the heart accepts God's will *even* in this, then she can live contentedly and make her handicap a pulpit for good.

Something else: don't let self-pity take over. Not for one moment! Ann faced many sorrows, problems, and heartaches, but never once did she indulge in self-pity. When she was tempted to, she began singing her favorite, "My Lord knows the way through the wilderness; All I have to do is follow."

God must love the widow. There are so many. According to statistics of the Metropolitan Life Insurance Company more than one-half million wives are widowed annually. Currently there are over eight million widows in the country.

MUST MAKE A LIVING

Mary writes, "I raised my five sons without a father. I hope and pray many times that I can stay at home instead of going out working. A widow's life is a hard road to travel, trying to make ends meet."

My heart goes out in pity, and in admiration, to such a mother. It isn't easy. I imagine that many a footsore, weary, lonely night she feels like giving up. But here is where faith gives her a lift—faith in the eternal God who can encourage, comfort and guide, that is, if she allows Him to.

Faith also in His promise, "If you seek Me first, and my will, I'll see to it that life's necessities will be supplied." Just ask Him for a job that won't separate you too much from the children.

Susan is custodian of her church. She knows what work is, but responds, "I do it joyfully and for God's glory, since He gave me my health."

Don't pity your children, if they don't have "everything" like their friends. Or if they need to get jobs and work hard too. Great men and women were not pampered, self-indulgent children.

CHILDREN RELATIONSHIPS

Furthermore, as you give yourself to the children, as you plan together and work together, as you co-operate and sacrifice for each other, the chances are that your family is closer knit than the family who has a father, but lacks the close harmony.

Try to daily incorporate those things like "Daddy did." Consciously carry out the plans and activities like you know he would have done them. Keep the children's memory freshened about their Daddy. Build up in them a healthy respect for him.

I admire Jane who said, "My husband ran away. . . . My job is very great for I must teach my boy (for his sake) to love and honor his father, even though his father doesn't seem to care for him."

A husbandless mother must be careful not to expect too much of her son, nor should she unduly pour out the affection upon her son which she would like to give to a husband.

A daughter's relationship with her mother will continue naturally, but she does miss her father's influence.

Realizing the need for the masculine influence Mary made it possible to spend weekends and special days at the home of her brother, who took a keen interest in the fatherless children. They, in turn, looked to him in respect and love. Together these families planned picnics and recreational fun.

Maybe you don't have a brother or a close relative who can partially fill in the gap. Surely there is some-one in your community—a teacher, scout leader, minister, or Sunday school teacher with whom the children can have happy associations.

A FULL SCHEDULE

The widow also needs to keep up her associates and friends as normally as possible. The temptation to withdraw from society must be shoved aside. She should continue attending the church, school, and community functions she normally attended. Remember, "If you want friends, you must make yourself friendly."

Kay had no children. After her husband's death she began working five days per week at a nursing home. Some patients are there because no one wants them. They feel life is a burden. So Kay tries to give them that "extra touch." In the morning she calls each one individually, by his or her name, adding a cheery, "Good morning." This followed by a word or two that is meant only for the individual, then a pat on the arm, or a tickle on the toe.

Kay says, "Just to see and hear each one respond is worth the extra time and concern."

If you don't need to earn the living, get involved in serving others. Help as an auxiliary member for the hospital, mental hospital or home for aged. Participate in church activities, mission societies, Red Cross activities. Cheer and read to the aged, or invalid neighbors. A young mother may desperately need a friend, someone to share with. The newcomer's children need a "grandmother."

Sue says when she gets lonely, she goes to the kitchen and bakes. Then she distributes the cookies and pastries to the neighborhood children and friends. Everyone enjoys freshly baked foods.

Should you be confined at home, you can write letters or cards to the burdened, the sad, or congratulations to those who achieve. Check your daily newspaper to learn of those ill, of marriages, births, deaths, or those involved in accidents, the discouraged, the ill. Keep a prayer list, and take time each day to pray for each request.

Also, keep up daily fellowship with Christ through prayer and Bible reading. Why not make your home the place for a cell group of women who study the Bible together and pray together.

Besides widows, there are the wives whose husbands are gone most of the day or all week or for longer periods.

This mother, too, must carry on alone. This calls for careful daily management, for all work to be done when he comes home. It means planning special family activities when he is at home. She too needs to keep the "father image" constantly before her children, instilling in them respect and loyalty to him. She will supervise writing letters to him, or plan projects for "Daddy to see." Above all, she must have right attitudes toward the separation. Attitudes rub off onto children, you know.

NOT ALONE

You are alone? No, not alone. Jesus Christ promises, "I will never leave you, nor forsake you."

Catherine Marshall says that God completely filled her life after her husband's death. His presence, His direct instructions and the added capacities He gave to her—these reassured her of His love and concern.

Face tomorrow bravely, "For God is already there." The widow with this faith and confidence walks on the inside of the sidewalk knowing that her divine Companion walks with her on the curb side. She consults her divine Partner in all her decisions. She talks over with Him each situation. Seeks His advice, His answer in every problem. She is at peace—her heart is still. She *knows* that He is God! She lives a life of trust!

Yes, maintain your circle of friends, your children's confidence and relationships. Fill your day with constructive activity. Become involved in helping others. But above all, remember your best friend, Jesus Christ. He sticks closer than a brother! He knows your every need. He has power to supply it. He is with you.

You are not alone!

13

A HEALTHY MIND

PSYCHIATRIST Franklin G. Ebaugh, writing in the *Pennsylvania Medical Journal,* says that "the universal disease of our time is anxiety," and millions of people are afflicted with emotional illness.

Many women (75% according to some doctors) frequent the doctor's office because they make themselves ill. Something in life has gone wrong. They can't cope with situations. They refuse to accept reality.

MODERN CULTURE

In the home, the modern woman is supposed to be wife, mother, laundress, nurse, cook, baker, diplomat, referee, plus leader in church and community activities. Probably we've been trained in outside activities, but most of us aren't adequately prepared for the responsibilities of wifehood and motherhood. And so the unknown, perhaps the unwanted, causes fear, brings tension and produces worry.

The changes in our culture are founded in the speed and pressure of living. New discoveries push us on into new horizons—yes, into space. But they've complicated our daily life.

In a newspaper article Dr. William C. Menninger, psychiatrist and president of the Menninger Foundation, Topeka, Kansas, states that there is "a direct relationship between this increased speed of living and the fact that we . . . have more people in mental hospitals than ever before."

HOSTILE FEELINGS

Dr. Menninger enlarges on this fact: "The key to good mental health is the ability to handle hostile feelings." He feels that in the laboratory of life— the home—we learn or don't learn to handle hostility. "But in our pace of living we don't take time to be kind, to show concern, to love. . . . There's no time for real communication between husband and wife, and consequently between parents and children. No time to compromise. . . . But harmonious relationships depend on making many compromises.

"Too busy for self-control. So we give vent to anger, to arguing, to pushing each other around."

LOVE IS NECESSARY

Dr. Menninger concludes that "the most important aspect in our personalities in terms of solving problems is the capacity to love, to care about other people . . . in the family and far beyond the borders of our own yards."

So, the healthy mind loves others. True love for every family member, for every neighbor, for all peoples can only come from knowing God because "God is love."

DISCIPLINED

The healthy mind is a disciplined mind.

Dr. Menninger says, "We must also provide controls for our children. There should be limits to behaviour in the home as elsewhere, and the limits should be identified. Children should not run a home."

This makes sense. It's reasonable. A disciplined and controlled child usually becomes an adult characterized by discipline.

A disciplined woman won't follow her moods. She won't wallow in wrong attitudes, thoughts of self-pity, fears, worry, hatred, grudges. She sets limits. She disciplines her thoughts and life.

FREE FROM GUILT

The healthy mind is free from guilt feelings. Self-condemnation, self-punishment, "I'm-no-good" feelings—these soon give way to unhealthy attitudes, to an unhealthy approach to self, to everyone else, and to life in general.

Unresolved sin not only weighs us down with guilt and wrong attitudes, but produces fear of people, of the future and of consequences. Fear produces tension and worry.

A woman bound up in guilt, fear and worry may escape reality through illness, alcoholism, drugs, unnecessary full-time job, excessive reading and viewing, overload of outside activities (even in *good* projects), pleasures. But sooner or later these escapes backfire, causing more fear and worry.

We all make mistakes, plenty of them. We all "have sinned," and missed God's perfect demands. But what you and I do with our guilt feelings makes the difference.

If I harbor them secretly and continually think about them, soon these guilt thoughts occupy too large a corner of my mind.

Only when I confess them singly and sincerely to God, and accept His forgiveness and "forgetness," only then I can forgive myself—and forget. God plainly says, "If we confess our sins, he is faithful . . . to forgive us our sins, and to cleanse us from all unrighteousness" (I John 1:9). "All" includes any and everything wrong.

OTHER PROBLEMS

But women also have other problems. Maybe your problem is jealousy of your husband, of the new neighbor.

A healthy mind will accept the accomplishments of others, and will congratulate them on their successes, even helping when possible.

Is your problem morning bedlam until husband and children get off to work and school? Then get up earlier, to allow adequate time for breakfast, for a short period of worship and prayer, for getting everyone off on time.

Are you afraid of new situations? Afraid of the

future in an atomic age? Afraid of death? Analyze your fears. Acquaint yourself with the facts. Face them squarely, with humor and a pleasant disposition.

Are you so wrapped up in extracurriculars that homemaking is pushed aside to a few nightly hours when you're all worn out and about ready to scream?

A woman with a healthy mind will put first things first. She will say no when necessary without being apologetic or torturing herself because she has refused.

PREVENTATIVE PSYCHIATRY

How can you maintain a healthy mind?

Dr. David M. Abrahamsen, a New York psychoanalyst, says, "You can learn a lot about your emotional reactions and your anxieties without consulting an expert. . . . You can do much for yourself in one hour every day of self-observation.

"By the time we are 20-25 we have certain opinions, certain feelings. The thing to do is to analyze these feelings, bring them to the surface."*

It's well to take time out to meditate, to think and to face ourselves.

It often helps to talk things out, to release the almost unbearable tensions by getting it out of your system. If something is making you tense, irritable, or keeping you awake at night, analyze the situation. Get it out into the open. Don't keep personal prob-

---

*"Hypochondriacs at Large," *Newskeek*, 23 (December 8, 1958), LII: 56.

lems cooped up inside yourself like a child's "ghost in the closet."

A TALK-IT-OVER

As homemaker, a talk-it-over with your husband, with a trusted friend, with a clergyman or with other homemakers will help.

But better yet, have a talk-it-over with Jesus Christ. He invites: "Come to me, you burdened and frustrated one . . . I will give you rest" (Matt. 11:28). Discuss in detail what's on your mind, whatever your problem, fear, worry or tension. After all, He knows *everything*. Do it with a thankful heart. You can always pull out at least one thing you enjoy and appreciate.

Allow Him to help you fill your mind with thoughts that are lovely, right, good, kind, honest, pure and beautiful. Then the peace of God will be with you. He will give you *rest!*

READ THE BIBLE

Get acquainted with God. Read the Bible so you can pull out a promise when you are afraid, angry, jealous, ill, tempted to worry. The Bible has something to say for each situation, disappointment, heartache or failure.

Betty had reached the point of a nervous breakdown. The doctor's brief prescription was: "Go home and read your Bible an hour a day . . . then come back to me a month from today."

At first Betty was angry. Then she decided that

the prescription was not an expensive one, so she'd give it a try.

In one month Betty went back to his office a different person.

Betty came very near refusing the remedy. But I believe, as this physician said: "There are many cases where, if tried, it would work wonders."

THE HEALTHY MIND

A woman with a healthy mind enjoys her tasks. She accepts reality. She looks beyond the immediate situation, beyond herself—to God. And by faith she accepts Him, His love, His words. She fits His words to her situation. She believes in prayer. She shows concern and love for others.

Let's remember the importance of the family, of the home—the maker or breaker of mental health. A home is where children should be prepared for life in a world of many people and many frustrations. Let your happy attitudes toward life rub off on your children. Teach them discipline and concern for others. Help them resolve hostile and guilt feelings. Let them know they are wanted and loved. Help them to have healthy minds.

14

THE TREASURES OF LEISURE

A NINE-YEAR-OLD GIRL, Mary Kraft, wrote a letter to a popular magazine. In it she complained that life was dull. She didn't know what to do with her leisure time. Well, Mary got plenty of suggestions. One stated, "Practice the hula hoop, if you have one." Mary wrote back, "I have a hula hoop, but I'm tired of that, too."

You're probably thinking, "Oh, if I only had some leisure time!"

Probably homemakers have less leisure time than anyone else. The homemaker needs to be on the job—cooking, cleaning, washing, ironing, loving and caring for husband and each child.

True, automation has entered her realm. Because of it she does have more available time—time not absolutely needed for housekeeping and mothering responsibilities. She is more and more aware of time-saving ways of doing housekeeping chores. She can often cut time in some areas without hindering the end results.

CONTROL LEISURE

And then when you accumulate a bit of leisure use it constructively. Consider the meaning of the word "leisure."

It originates from a Greek word with a dual meaning—(1) freedom from labor and (2) learning and discussing.

Lucy worked desperately hard, rushing through her morning housekeeping chores in order to have a few leisure moments in the afternoon. She buried herself in the latest serial or best seller. Yet, after an hour of this she felt defeated, not at all refreshed or eager to get back to her duties.

Lucy knew that a homemaker needs some leisure time, just for herself. What Lucy failed to recognize was that her spare time activities should leave her better able to cope with the daily demands as wife and mother. Her leisure time didn't do this but, on the contrary, made her dissatisfied with reality.

HAVE WORTHY GOALS

To be able properly to value leisure, as an individual or as a family, you first need to determine true values or true goals of living. There is no higher purpose or goal than to please and honor God and to serve others.

When you determine to accept this as your goal, then leisure won't be a problem. Rather, it will be a tool to enrich and to broaden your life.

Some of your leisure time you will want to spend

in meditating, collecting your thoughts, refreshing your mind to face the tensions of the day.

Leisure is a time you control. It should be a change of pace and attention. A time of recreation; not *wreckreation*. A time of relaxed service, creativeness and diversion.

You will want to enjoy leisure. That doesn't depend on what you do as much as why you do it.

If you crochet during leisure hours just to prove to neighbor Nancy that you can make as lovely an afghan as she can, then you can hardly enjoy crocheting.

What I'm trying to say is simply this: whatever your hobby, enjoy it. It will bring you joy and satisfaction only as you enter into it with the purpose of service and enjoyment, not to compete with someone.

Choose books, magazines, programs and entertainments that will make you a better wife, a better mother, a better friend and a better follower of Christ.

Maybe you prefer art or crafts or writing letters. You can pursue these with interest and with joy. The end results can be a blessing to you, to your family or to some friend.

Or try neighborliness in your leisure moments. Anna has caught this idea. Her family is grown— only one teen-age daughter at home. With today's automative household helps her new home requires little of her time and effort. So she's making good use of her leisure hours. One morning she enjoyed her flower-arranging class. One afternoon she visited the neighbor who had just returned from the hospital with her new baby. Several days later she invited the 18-year-old expectant mother, new in the neighborhood, over for a midmorning coffee snack. The girl was delighted to find a friend in her new location. Some afternoons Anna cheers aged folks at a nearby rest home.

WEALTH BRINGS LEISURE

Leisure has become a family matter. Automation, bringing about the 4-day work week, and increased wealth have brought about more leisure. Shorter days and weeks have become necessary to keep more men employed and employed longer. The traditional picture of the tired, bent toiler has been changed into the well-dressed, well-fed man with time on his hands.

In fact, the time may soon come when we will be faced with forced leisure—unemployment. According to a leading manufacturer of automation equipment, the time will soon come when automation will eliminate 40,000 jobs weekly.

The billions and billions of dollars spent annually by Americans for all types of entertainments—including sports, movies, hobbies, vacations—indicate leisure and wealth. Two billion dollars are spent yearly just on weekend recreation excursions. Reportedly we spend 30 percent of our days at play—and this does not include regular vacations!

We pity our forefathers with their problems—forced on them by unconquered soil and elements.

Too many of us believe work is only a necessary evil, to escape from whenever possible.

Tired, overworked peoples of other lands admire us. In fact, they envy us for our leisure time, entertainments and wealth. They imagine these to bring happiness. But this is not true. Leisure brings problems also, perhaps of greater extent, more complex and devastating than work.

PURPOSEFUL FAMILY LEISURE

You as a homemaker should also direct your family into purposeful creative use of their leisure hours.

And these hours don't have to be crammed with activities! Maybe what your youngsters long for more than anything else is an hour a day, or one evening a week, for time to be quiet, to slow down and think.

Your family must have time to share together, to be together. This can be done around the family table, through a leisure dinner hour. This helps develop family unity. It also helps prepare children for proper social behavior in later years.

A teen-age girl's club dinner turned out to be a disorderly occasion. Later one of the girls revealed one of the causes for it. She remarked, "At our house we never take time to sit down and eat together."

But I personally treasure those times when we, as a large family, used to sit around the table after finishing the meal. This usually occurred during the winter months—not daily, but occasionally.

Father would entertain with stories of when he was a boy, relating interesting adventures of his bicycling trips on Sundays, or when as a young horse trader he rode from Kansas to Pennsylvania on the boxcars, accompanying the horses.

On other occasions he shared experiences of his family, experiences of the church and Christian life.

At other times we'd engage in humorous activities: such as cutting a set of false teeth from an orange rind and fitting them into our mouths—maybe an upper, or a lower, or both. Or a cracker and peanut butter eating contest. Or making up stories—each one contributing a paragraph.

In another home, time is spent around the table relating interesting events of the day, sharing from each other's experiences, in discussing events and relating them to biblical truths.

HELPFUL ACTIVITIES

This is not time wasted. The satisfying activities of eating and conversing together are a unifying force for each family member.

Other leisure hours will be spent listening to wholesome programs and recordings, looking at family albums, reading, painting, visiting, picnics.

Candy-making is fast becoming a lost art in many homes. Cookie-baking, too. Why not round up your youngsters and revive these skills? Then share with an aged couple, the new neighbors and your friends.

Whatever you decide to do, enjoy the treasures of leisure. It isn't selfish to reach out and use your abilities in creative, helpful, satisfying activities. It contributes to more joyful living. It increases the joy you bring to others.

Your leisure hours can be meaningful treasures as you remember Christ's basic philosophy: Happiness and joy are by-products of giving self in loving service for others.

15

BE CONTENT

ARE YOU CONTENT?

Now be honest! When did you gripe last about those things beyond your control? You're too short, or too tall. You don't like the community you live in. You wish your husband would get a raise.

According to the dictionary, the word "content" is derived from a Latin word which means "to hold together." So, the basic meaning in the concept of contentment is not primarily satisfaction or resignation. It is being held together. This, of course, produces satisfaction.

To clarify this a bit more, let's think about the opposite—discontent. If you're discontent you're without content. You aren't holding together. You're disorganized.

If you are content you are organized. Your thoughts are holding together in the situation. You think clearly about the experience, or situation. You keep in focus the true values of life. Naturally, then, you talk and act in an organized way.

ACCEPT YOURSELF

You need to hold together, to be content, with yourself—with just who you are, with the unique personality, qualities, and talents God has assigned to you!

You are Mary, or Jane, or Shirley. Nobody else! You are a pianist, not an artist. You have blue eyes, not brown. Your hair is blonde, not dark. You keep organized as you accept yourself—your individual personality, your unique self. You hold your thoughts together about yourself.

In the words of Walt Whitman:

I exist as I am, that is enough;
If no other in the world be aware, I sit content,
And if each and all be aware, I sit content.
One world is aware, and by far the largest to
    me, and that is myself;
And whether I come to my own to-day, or in
    ten thousand or ten million years,
I can cheerfully make it now, or with equal
    cheerfulness I can wait.

You exist as you are. So—accept yourself. Be content.

NOBLE DISCONTENT

Yet, after having said this, I must clarify a bit. In some areas you should not be content. You should never be satisfied with the status quo, with situations that should be changed.

You'll never want to be content with social conditions such as poverty, war, discrimination, ill will, greed, graft, hate, vice. Your lack of love, lack of kindness, or your child's illness won't allow you to be content and do nothing to remedy the situation.

In the words of James Russell Lowell:

> This life were brutish did we not sometimes
> Have intimations clear of wider scope,
> Hints of occasion infinite, to keep
> The soul alert with noble discontent
> And onward yearnings of unstilled desire. . . .

I like the words "noble discontent." That, I think, not only includes a discontent of social conditions around you, but also a discontent with yourself as you relate to God and your fellowmen. An undercurrent of discontent should drive you on to be a kinder, more understanding wife. A happier, more loving, more patient, more forgiving mother. To be more efficient as a homemaker, a sweeter neighbor and a more obedient follower of Jesus Christ.

However, in order to be happy you do need an attitude of contentment with those circumstances you cannot change. Daily you need to pray as did St. Francis of Assisi:

> God, grant me the serenity
> To accept the things I cannot change,
> The courage to change the things I can,
> And the wisdom
> To know the difference!

Now, I want to apply this in a practical way.

TRUE VALUES

Are you content with your husband? His income? When you are tempted to envy your neighbor's home, her talents, or her husband, recall your husband's love, his faithfulness. William Shakespeare said:

For thy sweet love remember'd such wealth brings
That then I scorn to change my state with kings.*

Riches and wealth do not consist necessarily of money, or things. Neither does contentment depend on them. To be content with what you have is the greatest of all riches!

CONTRAST

Mary wasn't content! She made herself and everyone else uncomfortable with her constant complaining. She compared her children with others. She failed to accept their failures and to acknowledge their successes. Her husband was too quiet. She wanted him to be more aggressive. She couldn't live on his salary of 10,000 dollars because she always bought more than was on her shopping list, and opened unnecessary charge accounts.

Quite a contrast to Mrs. K. She and her husband, in their seventies, have a monthly income and security which totals $240. They pay $90 rent, besides many medical bills. And inflation has caught them. But instead of complaining, instead of demanding

---

*William Shakespeare, "Sonnet XXIX," *The Love Poems and Sonnets of William Shakespeare* (Garden City, N. Y.: International Collectors Library, American Headquarters, 1957), p. 23.

that society owes them more, they are content. They are holding together. But they've had to do some adjusting. They now eat only two slices of bacon a day. They are careful about prices. They note a dollar difference on an item. Mr. K. gets a haircut once a month, instead of every two or three weeks.

Mrs. K. wants two new living room chairs badly, but comments, "If we get them, I'll be satisfied, but if we don't get them, I'll be satisfied. We're going to stand on our own as long as we can, even if we do without a lot of things."

There's a contented woman! Satisfied within her situation. Holding herself together, not blaming her husband for not having provided a nest egg for old age, not complaining because society doesn't hand over all she desires.

This reminds me of a motto my niece says hangs above their kitchen sink. (She comes from a family of nine.)

> Eat it up,
> Wear it out.
> Make it do,
> Or do without.

This must have been Mrs. K.'s motto!

We parents, especially mothers, need to be examples of contentment for our children.

Contentment brings happiness, an inner joy and peace of mind. It frees your mind for positive, worthwhile thoughts and actions.

GRATITUDE

The contented woman is grateful for what she does have, not griping about what she lacks. Gratitude is the foundation upon which contentment builds.

This is the way it works. Instead of griping because of something you don't have or can't do, you bring to mind something you have or can do or enjoy.

RESULTS OF DISCONTENT

Discontent often leads to unnecessary demands and excessive installment buying. This in turn may lead to husband moonlighting and family troubles. Kate complained about her house until Tom bought a new one. Then he took on two jobs to meet the payments. He was never home. Kate was alone with the children. Then she got tired of this. Two years later she became infatuated with the 18-year-old boy next door. She got a divorce from Tom and married the youth.

In Gail's case she got a job to pay for the new dining room and living room suites—which they didn't really need. But the children were neglected. Today they run wild. The parents are heartbroken. These tragic situations—a broken home, frustrated children—because Mom was discontent!

Benjamin Franklin says, "Content makes poor men rich; discontent makes rich men poor."

CONTENTMENT IS LEARNED

Basically, contentment is learned.
We as a family have gone through many changes.

And you'll not doubt my word about the many changes, when I tell you that in fourteen years we moved eleven times! After each move, I felt defeated and discouraged, simply because I envisioned immediate contentment in the changing experience. I'd often refer to St. Paul's confession, "I have learned in whatever situation I am to be content."

Finally, after many years, I discovered the phrase, "I have learned." It hit me like a thunderbolt. He *learned*. It was not an instantaneous experience! Although he didn't say whether he learned in one day, in two weeks, or in two years, the important truth was that he learned.

Well, this discovery changed my attitude. I too have learned and am learning to accept each new situation, however difficult or rewarding. Some of us learn more slowly than others, but thank God we learn! And that's what counts!

Take a good look at your gripes. Analyze them. Face reality. Focus on true values of life. Accept God's concern and interest in you. Hold together, organizing your thoughts. Then learn to fit yourself into the situations. If there's no need to change, just accept them and be content.

16

ON WINGS OF PRAYER

IN RELATING HER STRUGGLES as a widow with two children Ann says: "Often I would go alone in my room, on my knees and with eyes full of tears. I prayed to God about my failures as a mother, about the children growing up without a father, and about all their needs. And God was always faithful."

Her daughter just finished nurse's training and her son is attending college. Although they don't know their earthly father, they experience happy relationships with their heavenly Father. Because Mother knew Him and depended on Him.

ACKNOWLEDGES DEPENDENCE

Prayer simply acknowledges that we do depend on God . . . that there are some needs we cannot meet alone, some demands we are unable to fulfill with our own wisdom or resources. That's what prayer says—we need God. Just as a child needs to share his thoughts and wishes with his earthly father, we need to talk things over with God.

Jesus *wants* you to come to Him. "Ask and you shall receive."

PRAYER THAT SUCCEEDS

But preface your prayers with adoration, praise and thanksgiving. Take time out to meditate on who God is. Pull out at least one thing you can thank Him for. Even if you think there's absolutely nothing good in your life or circumstances, praise Him for salvation, for sins forgiven, for peace of mind, for the hope of heaven where there's no more pain, sorrow or death.

Next comes confession. Mention those sins that sort of muddy up your mind—those unkind, ugly, critical thoughts about your neighbor, your hubby, or your child. Mention those words and acts that have hurt God and others. Confess them. Yes, every one. Ask for forgiveness. And then He forgives you your wrongdoings as you forgive those who have wronged you.

Keep the channel between you and God clean and open. Several weeks ago I connected my electric sweeper but it just wouldn't pick up the dirt. So I detached the hose and shook it but nothing came out. Next I put in a short rod, and shook again. Sure enough, out came the rod plus a silk scarf. Well, with the obstruction gone, the air got through the hose and suction was restored. In the same way, God's power and blessings cannot get through to you as long as the connection is clogged.

Next remember that you will receive when you ask according to God's will. You ask and probably have not because you ask selfishly, to gratify your wants! Pray in the attitude of "Thy will be done" and you will receive.

Prayer is also listening to God who reveals His will, helping you sort out your needs from wants!

THE BEST FRIEND

Prayer is a lifting of the heart and mind to God. Speak frequently to Him in your own words about your joys and sorrows, successes and failures, and you'll develop great wisdom and understanding.

Now, you're ready to ask for your own personal needs. Tell Him about the housekeeping routine, the sick baby, the nosy neighbor. Ask specifically. Pray in times of temptation and victory. Pray for your children while they are at school. Thank God the courts can't rule that out!

Jesus is your closest friend. He cares. There's nothing too big, too little, or too embarrassing to discuss with Him. After all, He already knows everything.

INTERCESSORY PRAYERS

Your prayers should also include needs and problems of others—your husband, each child, the neighbors, and friends, even your enemies, and those people in special service for God. Acquaint yourself with their needs. Be specific. Detail their desires and needs. Then God can use you in time of emergency.

Dick Hillis reports that as a young missionary to China he was completely discouraged, ready to give up. One day he was on his knees, battling with God.

Finally he ceased his struggle and accepted the promise that God would see him through.

At the same time, in Pasadena, California, a little woman was suddenly awakened at midnight with a feeling she should pray. She tried to shrug it off, but couldn't. As she scanned her alphabetical prayer list she came to the name of a young missionary in China. She had never met him, but had seen his picture in a missionary magazine, and faithfully remembered him in prayer daily. Now she had this burden for him. She didn't know his need. So she prayed, "Dear God, see him through." That man was Dick Hillis.

Yes, make your prayer list for others. Pray for them daily if possible, and whenever God brings an individual name to mind, don't brush it off. Bring it to God in prayer. I personally have marveled at the way God answers my prayers for others in this way. It has increased my faith in God and prayer.

THANK GOD FOR ANSWERS

When God answers, then be sure to thank Him.

In their growing years it was often difficult to keep our boys in clothes. One fall Martin needed trousers and shoes. We had been praying that God would supply the money for them. Then unexpectedly a patron on his paper route told him to go to the store and pick out trousers and shoes for his Christmas gift. She had not known of our prayer. Later as I told her and her husband that this was an answer to prayer they reminded me, "Mrs. Miller, be sure and thank the Lord for His answer." Yes, a thank you to God is important.

I was amazed to read recently that the South African government called for a day of fasting and prayer for rain. Then when rains came, the government proclaimed a day of national thanksgiving!

ANSWERS DIFFERENTLY

God sometimes answer with "no," but He answers. His all-knowing mind recognizes the wrong requests. A small child sees big brother using a sharp knife. He wants it too. But is denied it. That's the way God has to do sometimes.

Sometimes God answers with, "Wait, you're not quite ready to receive this."

But when you know your request is within God's will, then "pray without ceasing." Pray. Don't quit until the answer comes. One woman prayed seventeen years before her husband accepted Jesus Christ, and was changed from a drunkard to a saint of God.

WOMEN OF PRAYER

A few minutes ago a call came over the phone to pray for a couple that's really having a rough time. After several months of separation they're together again. He quit his drinking. They seemed happy. But something ruffed him up and he's on a drinking spree again. But we're going to pray until victory comes.

Several years ago our church women started a prayer chain—each one of us calls a designated person who in turn calls someone else. That way in a very short time many women are notified and united prayers begin. And God answers!

I believe that women can serve God and humanity best through devoted lives of faith and prayer. To be sure, God often uses them to answer their own prayers.

YOU CAN PRAY

You say, "But, Ella May, I can't pray!" I ask you, "Can you converse with another woman?" Then you can talk to God—that's what prayer is. You only learn to pray by praying.

You could never learn to knit by simply reading the directions. No, you'll need to loop the yarn over the knitting needle and get started. And the more you knit the easier it becomes. The same is true of prayer.

You say, "I'm too busy to pray!" What foolish words! They say you can get along without God!

> Away with work that hinders prayer
> 'Twere best to lay it down,
> For prayerless work, however good,
> Will fail to win the crown.

Surely you can find a few minutes as you retire, or as you get up in the morning, or a 10-or 15-minute break when the children are napping. But that's not enough. You can pray as you perform routine tasks, as you wait at the stop light, or if sleep comes slowly. You need to pray! "Prayer changes things!"

You can reach the heart of God. You can fly above troubles, housekeeping frustrations and temptations —on wings of prayer!

PROOF

If radio's slim fingers
Can pluck a melody
From night and toss it over
A continent or sea;
If the petaled white notes
Of a violin
Are blown across a mountain
Or a city's din;
If songs, like crimson roses,
Are culled from the thin blue air,
Why should mortals wonder
That God hears and answers prayer?

ETHEL ROMIG FULLER

17

WHAT IS HAPPINESS?

TO THE AMERICAN INDIAN the recipe for perpetual happiness was a trip to the "happy hunting grounds" where he could hunt, dance and gamble forever. To the Buddhist happiness is Nirvana, a blissful state of emptiness free of all desire, and he'll spend not only one lifetime trying to achieve it, but several!

Happiness in the opinion of a famous beauty was a mink coat and a Nedick's hotdog eaten on Broadway at midnight. A Greek philosopher promised his king that he would be happy as soon as he found a happy man and put on his shirt. (As it happened, when the king found the happy man, the man didn't have a shirt.)

The poet Wordsworth said that to be happiest, you should be in love. Jeremy Taylor believed knowledge brought happiness. And Jefferson said that happiness is the result of a good conscience!

And then there are the people who think clams are happiest. You've heard the expression, "happy as a clam." The Japanese have named suicide by disemboweling "happy dispatch" (hara-kiri). Then there are those who consider an obsession a form of happiness—"ski happy," "club happy."

OUT OF REACH

Ask five women what happiness is, and you'll likely have five different answers.

The poor woman will say, "Happiness is having all the money I want."

The single woman will reply, "Happiness is a husband and family."

The aged woman will answer, "Happiness is being less than thirty."

The uneducated woman will say, "Happiness is a degree, used in a career."

However, the educated woman may respond, "Happiness is being an aborigine who has never heard of equality, committees or nuclear warfare."

You see, happiness is getting that which fills a known need.

To the lonely woman, happiness is companionship. To the tired woman, happiness is rest. To the tense woman, pressured by daily homemaking demands, happiness is getting away from it all—perhaps a vacation.

Happiness cannot be sought and found for its own sake, nor as an end. It is something like a butterfly; when pursued it's just beyond your reach. However, if you sit down quietly, it may light upon you.

WRONG PURSUIT OF HAPPINESS

As elusive as happiness seems to be, you and I desire it. The "pursuit of happiness" is the third of our three "inalienable" rights granted in the American Declaration of Independence. Now, just how well are we doing it?

A few years ago *Life* magazine brought together a panel of eighteen men and women to discuss this question for public benefit.

These experts represented leadership in all of the major fields of human interest. Opinions differed on certain particulars, but on this they agreed—that Americans tend to fool themselves. They think they are happier than they really are.

One basis for such a conclusion was the fact that America's liquor bill, nine billion dollars per year, is three times the amount of its school bill. Is this an intelligent demonstration of the right to pursue happiness?

GOD-PERMITTED

Are you exercising your right to search for happiness? Yours—for the seeking and the winning. Not free. Happiness is the result, the product, of endeavor.

I'm so glad this is true, aren't you? God permits you to find happiness if you look in the proper places for it. Joseph Salak says, "Most people in the pursuit of happiness are in such a rush they pass it right by." Happiness doesn't come from easy work, but from the afterglow of satisfaction coming from the achievement of a difficult task that demanded your best. It comes not from doing what you like, but from liking what you do.

Charles Kingsley said, "We act as if comfort and luxury were the chief requirements of life, when all that we need to make us really happy is something to be enthusiastic about." This is in sharp contrast to today's philosophy that you'll find happiness as you run away from your responsibilities.

Today's twentieth century approach to happiness should be a down-to-earth kind of way.

Find happiness in what you have, instead of thinking it's in what you don't have. Like Dale Carnegie says, "When you have lemons, make lemonade."

IN SMALL THINGS

Pull out happiness from the situation in which you find yourself, and from the little things surrounding you. A little girl found this. In her essay, "My Twelve Loveliest Things, People Not Counted," she lists:

"The scrunch of dry leaves as you walk through them; the feel of clean clothes; water running in the bath; the cool of ice cream; cool wind on a hot day; climbing up and looking back; honey in your mouth; smell of a drugstore; hot water bottle in bed; babies smiling; the feeling inside when you sing; baby kittens."

A homemaker expresses her happiness in the poem:

HOMEMADE HAPPINESS

Posies on the window sill
Wafting perfume lightly.
Yellow canary starts to trill
Sweet and shrill and spritely.
A white, bright wash gaily flapping;
A freshly scrubbed kitchen floor;
A spicy apple pie baking,
A neighborly knock at the door.
A husband's smile; a youngster's yell.
A baby's hug and soft, moist kiss
Put them all together—they spell
To the homemaker, HAPPINESS!

THOUGHT-SHIFTING

Another famous twentieth century recipe for happiness is the thought-shifting process. You didn't get the new rug—or a meringue fell. Instead of wailing over it, do something nice at once that will make someone else happy. Send that long-put-off letter, bake your husband a cake, buy an extra paper from the newsboy. The theory here is that the happiness you give will bounce back and cheer you up.

Yet another modern approach to the production of happiness is the key-word method of happy relaxation. Here's how that works.

Find a set of eight words that make you relax and smile—your favorite niece or favorite song. Have a hobby? Choose a favorite incident, a favorite success perhaps, and find the key word that subconsciously brings it sweeping back. A set of these words supposedly works as subconscious mechanical levers to produce happiness when happiness seems very far away.

CHEMICAL CONTROL

And science offers easier solutions yet to the pursuit of happiness. "Happiness pills" that depress your depressions are one, and they are currently tinkering hard with the theory that chemicals control our moods and emotions.

Food faddists take this a step further, and say that happiness depends on good eating habits. Their premise is that if you will feed your body the right raw materials (foods) it will manufacture happiness almost wholesale in its own marvelous little chemical plants.

SOMETHING TO HOPE FOR

Perhaps the greatest reason for happiness is having something to hope for. The Bible says: "Blessed [happy] is the man . . . whose hope the Lord is" (Jer. 17:7).

Real happiness comes in forgetting self. You forget self as you get interested in Jesus Christ. As you fix your eyes, your goals and your mind on Him, then you see beyond daily incidents. You see beyond sorrow, pain, loss and heartaches. You see Him! He also helps you to see others, to find something to do for them. And if there's no one on this earth you have as your own to love—you have Him.

You are not out seeking joy. No, joy comes to you

as a fruit, a natural product of just being a branch on the True Vine. "The fruit of the Spirit is . . . joy," is happiness.

That's not all. The Bible says: "If in this life only we have hope in Christ, we are of all men most miserable" (I Cor. 15:19).

What is this hope beyond present life that brings joy? It's the hope of final perfection, of complete salvation in Jesus Christ. Salvation from all sin and evil. Salvation from all sorrow, pain and disappointments. Salvation from all unkindness, tension and frustration. Salvation will be complete as we join Christ in the endless years.

This hope brings joy? Let's explain it this way. Your child is away from home. He overcomes much of his loneliness and disappointments, as he thinks about the day when he will be home with you. This hope helps keep him happy. In a similar way, the hope in a future with Christ brings happiness! It keeps us centered on Him.

In knowing Christ true happiness can be yours! Right now! Right at home! In whatever circumstance you may find yourself.

Mary Hamlett Goodman incorporates a big truth in this little verse:

> I can be about as happy
> As I make up my mind to be;
> For it's not so much what happens
> As what's in the heart of me!